# MANIFESTING MICHELANGELO

# MANIFESTING MICHELANGELO

The True Story of a Modern-Day
Miracle—That May Make
All Change Possible

JOSEPH PIERCE FARRELL
*with* PETER OCCHIOGROSSO

**ATRIA** PAPERBACK
NEW YORK   LONDON   TORONTO   SYDNEY   NEW DELHI

**ATRIA** PAPERBACK
A Division of Simon & Schuster, Inc.
1230 Avenue of the Americas
New York, NY 10020

First Atria Paperback hardcover edition November 2011

**ATRIA** PAPERBACK and colophon are trademarks of Simon & Schuster, Inc.

For information about special discounts for bulk purchases,
please contact Simon & Schuster Special Sales at 1-866-506-1949
or business@simonandschuster.com.

The Simon & Schuster Speakers Bureau can bring authors to your live event.
For more information or to book an event, contact the Simon & Schuster Speakers Bureau
at 1-866-248-3049 or visit our website at www.simonspeakers.com.

*Designed by Diane Hobbing of Snap-Haus Graphics*

Manufactured in the United States of America

10   9   8   7   6   5   4   3   2   1

The Library of Congress has cataloged the hardcover edition as follows:

Farrell, Joseph Pierce.
Manifesting Michelangelo : the true story of a modern-day miracle—that may make
all change possible / Joseph Pierce Farrell; with Peter Occhiogrosso.—
1st Atria Books hardcover ed.
p. cm.
1. Farrell, Joseph Pierce. 2. Healers—United States—Biography.
3. Consciousness. I. Occhiogrosso, Peter. II. Title.
RZ408.F37A3 2011
615.8'52'092—dc22          2010023464
[B]

ISBN 978-1-4391-7301-5
ISBN 978-1-4391-7302-2 (pbk)
ISBN 978-1-4391-7303-9 (ebook)

Beauteous art, which, brought with us from heaven,
will conquer nature; so divine a power.

—*Michelangelo*

# CONTENTS

## PART I: THE PATH OF DISCOVERY

# PART II: THE FIVE STEPS

# An Invitation

*You have never heard of me. This is the true story of a person being born without the advantages of privilege, pedigree, or wealth who one day, with the undiminished imagination of a child, attempted the impossible and succeeded, and in doing so discovered a latent human potential that transformed his life.*

*The inheritance that we are all born with, the potential that resides beyond the perceptions of our five senses and the measure of science, if ignited, will empower you with the capacity to literally transform yourself, your life, and the world around you. It is my hope that this book will inspire you to embark on the Five Step path to ignite your sacred potential to manifest the life you were born to live.*

*Be not afraid, the path to realize your potential is not an intellectual pursuit. I was labeled an "underachiever" in school and was advised by my guidance counselor to set my goals "a bit lower" and to abandon my dreams. However, as you will soon read, my soul rebelled and had a different plan in store.*

*As I searched for the highest and best use for my life, I read the stories of the most beloved people throughout time, those individuals who have been placed in the pantheon of greatness by the citizenry. The names of Washington, Wilberforce, the Wright brothers, Gandhi, Mandela, King, Salk, and Parks all came to mind. As I read their stories, I realized that all of their journeys had five common steps.*

*They all looked around, seeing challenges, obstacles, and ignorance; decided to make a change; connected to a higher source; and acted;*

*and their actions* manifested *in the world and became legend. Their legacies are gifts to humanity that have inspired people with gratitude for generations.*

*This book is my personal invitation to you. It was not written to awe you but to inspire you, to encourage each and every one of you to ignite that latent ember of potential that rests within you.*

*Now, perhaps more than at any time in history, the world needs inspired women, men, and children working in all fields if we are to overcome the challenges that confront humanity today. It is my hope that you will embark on the five-step path to ignite your great potential and manifest your own masterpiece for the benefit of yourself, your family, and your larger family, humanity.*

*Who knows? If you look around, decide to manifest a change, connect to a higher source, and then act, you may just find yourself sitting next to your peers in the pantheon of greatness!*

—Joseph Pierce Farrell

The good that men do is small in amount compared with what men and women bear locked in their hearts . . . to unbind what is bound, to bring the underground waters to the surface, humanity is waiting and longing.

—*Albert Schweitzer*

# FOREWORD

When Joseph Pierce Farrell first approached me to write the fore-
word for this book, I was more than receptive for a number of
reasons. First, I have come to recognize and respect Joseph as a
visionary and bridge builder in the study of science and spirituality. One day, after having completed five surgeries, I picked up
my wife and drove to a formal dinner being held in Manhattan in
honor of a titled dignitary. Attending this party were leaders in
politics, medicine, and science, in addition to European nobility.

I had heard about Joseph's work months earlier from friends
and colleagues who recommended that I meet him because of our
similar areas of interest. I am a Georgetown University Medical
School graduate who went on to become a board-certified urologist and have maintained an active clinical practice for twelve years.
I initially chose to practice medicine because I felt it would be the
highest and best way for me to help people. Within the Hippo-
cratic Oath there are specific tenets pertaining to the ethical practice of medicine. Inherent in this agreement is the pledge to do
no harm by way of sins of commission or omission. Given that,
I am continually seeking efficacious modalities that can help my
patients. Although practicing medicine is a noble pursuit, I became
disenchanted when I found in it a bias and a focus in medicine that
weighed heavily in favor of advancing certain areas at the expense
of omitting other areas worthy of exploration. Propelled to discover alternatives, I found myself traveling in Asia and South Amer-

ica, where I encountered physicians and healthcare providers with a common goal to explore various modalities in the hope of finding efficacious techniques to complement modern clinical care.

Ironically, it wasn't until I returned to the United States that I met Joseph and found what I had been searching the globe for. Here was a man in conventional attire who was said to possess the capacity to work at the same level as legendary healers in South America as well as avatars from India. The passion with which I'd entered medicine was rekindled after I encountered another person who shared my passion for advancing the boundaries of healthcare beyond their current limits.

The following week I received an invitation to join the cross-disciplinary team of physicians and scientists who were engaged in research at the Global Health Institute. As I observed Joseph work, through my scientific, clinical eyes, my perception permanently shifted. I witnessed the effective intervention of a modality not known by Western medicine. Joseph was transforming human tissue, through intention, within a matter of minutes. A patient came in with a lateral malrotation of the right leg and severe swelling of the ankle. In fifteen minutes the ankle experienced complete absence of swelling and the medial malleolus (ankle bone) previously not seen became visible. The patient's foot and leg were straightened.

I continued to review Joseph's work and have been present for a number of sessions where participants in observational studies have had work done. These individuals had previously been cared for by physicians at some of the highest level institutions in the New York City area and were told nothing further could be done for them. I have seen dramatic improvements in both the physical and psychological states of participants who have had the benefit of Joseph's intervention. We were actively engaged in the exploration of consciousness and its relationship to health and healing.

Despite the demands on my time, including being the founding Board member and managing partner of a kidney stone treatment center with a staff of one hundred, as well as a full-time practicing surgeon and father to a newborn, I was compelled to join a team of professionals engaged in developing the currently emerging integrative health model.

What I witnessed in Joseph's work was not "thinking" similar to what I had been exposed to in the scientific medical field for the past thirteen years. I knew I had seen something extraordinary. I recalled scientists of the nineteenth century who studied the wings of birds and soon thereafter unlocked their mystery and created the new branch of science known as aviation. In the twentieth century, wishing to enable aircraft to fly at night, scientists studied bats and discovered radar. In the twenty-first century, the physicists who harness ineffable energies will give to humanity something sublime.

It is my belief that rigorous scientific exploration of the benevolent source working through Joseph will shape the new healthcare model of this millennium and the future of medicine. It is my opinion that, given the advances in biophysics that support these modalities, linked with the demands of patients for integrative and complementary care, medicine will begin to embrace the notion of consciousness and spirit as mediators of material and thus physical change.

*Frank T. Salvatore, M.D.*
*Chair, Medical Advisory Board,*
*Global Health Institute, 2006–2009*

The significant problems we face cannot be solved at the same level of thinking we were at when we created them.

—*Albert Einstein*

# PART I

## THE PATH OF DISCOVERY

## Chapter 1

## HIDING IN PLAIN SIGHT

*If you bring forth what is within you,*
*what you have will save you. . . .*
*—Gospel of Thomas, Saying 70*

It was January 2000, the dawn of a new millennium, and change
was in the air. It was also a time when people around the world,
individually and collectively, paused for a moment to look inside
and question who they were, how far they had progressed, and
where they were heading. I was no exception.

Like many of those who made the pilgrimage to New York
City in the early 1980s in search of material success, I had come
ashore in the midst of a circus of decadence and compulsive
spending. Wall Street had hoodwinked a nation into believing
that greed was good, and people were outdoing one another to
see who could be the best. This was especially true in the world
of real estate and finance, where I had chosen to take my shot at
the wheel of life. My childhood dream was to pursue a career in
healthcare, to help restore people's lives, but my high school guidance counselor had delivered the painful news that, at least on

3

paper, I was a classic underachiever who simply didn't live up to his potential. In his opinion, I should abandon my dream of working in healthcare.

Instead, I followed my dad's advice and spent four years training as a cadet midshipman in the U.S. Maritime Administration, with summers spent sailing around the globe. In my free time, I followed in the wake of the friendly ship's physician, watching him patch up the sailors and getting vicarious satisfaction as a student medical corpsman. I followed that with two years of business classes while I broke into the highly competitive field of New York City real estate. Having learned to navigate the seas, I now knew how to avoid the two-legged variety of sharks who infested the waters of Manhattan. In the process, I'd suffered a few bites and paid my dues, which amounted to several chunks taken out of my soul, but I had survived and begun to prosper materially.

Like many of the people in the city, each morning I donned a suit and tie, then walked the ten blocks south from my small apartment on the Upper East Side to my office. On the way, I passed the Manhattan Eye, Ear, and Throat Hospital, where some of the top reconstructive surgeons in the nation restored the faces of disfigured children and adults. Combining their medical training with a fundamental grasp of the art of sculpting, they dressed in surgical aprons and wielded an array of scalpels, saws, fine chisels, and rasps to undo the harm that nature or humanity had visited upon their patients. I couldn't avoid seeing kids exiting cars or walking from the nearby subway station, their faces, ears, or noses bandaged after surgical procedures to correct some trauma brought about by automobile accidents, burns, or genetic disorders. Their faces and heads were often covered in an attempt to avoid the inevitable stares and painful taunts of the groups of more fortunate children en route to and from several schools in the area.

My heart always went out to these kids and their parents. I wasn't aware of it at the time, but the feelings that were registering within me were the keys to unearthing my subconscious desires—my childhood dream of a career in healthcare, which still lay dormant like a seed buried in my soul and would flash to the surface whenever I happened to pass any scene of a car crash, an injured pedestrian, or any other apparent suffering. But seeing those kids trying to conceal their disfigurement made me feel especially impotent that I couldn't do anything to help.

So, when I strolled through the impressively appointed lobby of my Madison Avenue office, the reflection of my uniform of a business suit and the click of the heels of my comfortable Italian loafers on the marble floor provided little solace for my lack of enthusiasm toward the role I played as J. P. Farrell, Investment Consultant and Appraiser of Real Property. Blah, blah, blah. It was a soulless job consisting of coordinating with real estate brokers, banks, and mortgage lenders to smooth the paths of the corporate executives and affluent individuals arriving in New York daily to buy into the dream of material nirvana. I was all but unaware of why my life had started to disintegrate, although the symptoms were plain to see: I was despondent and had lost weight; an open smile was gone from my face, replaced by an empty mask. I had lost all interest in my work, and the doctor I saw in desperation diagnosed my condition as dysthymia, a low-grade depression.

One Saturday morning in this frame of mind, I dragged myself to Peter's Barber Shop for a much needed haircut. Recently I had begun to neglect little things like personal grooming, and my friends had mentioned that I was looking a bit disheveled, just another sign of my creeping malaise. While I was waiting my turn for the barber, I picked up *The New York Times* and read a story about the discovery a few decades before of twelve leather-bound papyrus manuscripts buried in sealed jars that an Egyptian peasant farmer had stumbled upon while searching for fertilizer in the mountains close to his village. Afraid that the tall, ancient vessels might contain evil genies, the young man hesitated to open them, but the lure of hidden gold got the better of him, and he cracked open the pots with his tools. Indeed, a cloud of golden dust appeared, but as it settled the farmer reached in and discovered that the vessels contained not gold but simply some old, decaying scrolls.

Not realizing that he had unearthed a priceless treasure forgotten for nearly two thousand years, he brought home the papyrus to use as fuel in his oven. Eventually the manuscripts that escaped becoming oven fodder were sold on the black market, then rescued by an Egyptian museum. When their translation was completed in the 1970s, they were found to contain lost secret teachings that came to be known as the Gnostic Gospels. As I grew increasingly fascinated by the account, the barber called me away from my Indiana Jones reverie and invited me to sit in his chair.

While he snipped away, I continued to wonder what was in those documents, why they had been carefully sealed and hidden by holy men so many centuries ago. My mood lifted somewhat, buoyed by the possibility of mysteries beyond my scope of knowledge. The following Monday, however, after suffering through an excruciatingly boring lunch with some business execs who fancied themselves "masters of the universe," my malaise returned in full force. I was passing a Barnes & Noble on my way home from work when I saw the cover of the book mentioned in the newspaper article: a selection of texts from the Gnostic Gospels. Excited, I walked inside to see if it was really true that heretofore unknown wisdom could be purchased for a few dollars. I bought a copy of the text, and that evening I began to read it. As

I read, it seemed as if these words were reaching through time to present me with a personal message:

If you bring forth what is within you,
what you have will save you.
If you do not bring it forth,
what you do not have within you will kill you.

Right then the serendipitous arrival of wisdom that had been buried for many centuries resonated in me, not in my head but in my heart. And somehow, in a way I couldn't explain, it activated my dormant childhood dreams. Having stumbled along an uninspiring path during the intervening years, I now made the decision to alter my course, to bring forth what was within me—lest the failure to do so kill me.

Suddenly it was as if new breath coursed through my body. I woke up the next day with a bounce in my step and wind in my sails. I practically skipped to work, so great was my eagerness to resign my joyless job and start a new life—although what exactly that life would be, I couldn't have told you. Without any new work lined up, or any sure course of action, I was jumping without a net. My decision may have defied logic and rationality, but it gave my heart and soul a tremendous feeling of liberation.

Chapter 2

# KNOCKING ON HEAVEN'S DOOR

The most beautiful and profound emotion we can experience is the sensation
of the mystical.
—Albert Einstein

As the weeks went by and my bills started to pile up, I realized that
I would need to find some source of income to keep me going
until I decided which field of healthcare I would enter. When I
walked down to the Garden Deli on the corner of Seventy-first
Street in Manhattan, I noticed a sign on the landing in front of a
shop: INTERIOR DESIGN & DECORATING. Beneath that were the words
"Transforming Ordinary into Extraordinary" and "Old World
craftsmanship."

The words appealed to me on a deep level. As a child, I had
watched my dad, who was extremely handy with tools, build
and repair all sorts of things. My mother ran a ceramics studio in
our basement, where she taught local women, and she had conveyed to me the skills of shaping clay and painting and preparing
a wide assortment of finishes. After our family moved from New

York City to the suburbs of Long Island, I picked up the craft of boat repair from some Norwegian boat builders there. Whatever genetic aptitude I'd inherited from my parents seemed to stand me in good stead whenever I set my hands and heart to working with wood. Maybe this shop could use a skilled workman to help repair and restore antiques. Thinking I had nothing to lose, I rang the bell and went into the office. When I told the owner that I was interested in part-time work, he asked me to tell him a little about myself.

I mentioned my nautical and business training and my lack of enthusiasm for the real estate work I'd been doing. When I came to the part about quitting to pursue my longtime dream of a career in healthcare, I caught a flash of recognition in the owner's knowing smile. He informed me that he had attended medical school himself but ironically had departed to pursue his calling in interior design. We seemed like a good fit.

"Well," he said at last, "what can you do? Can you work with wood?"

I said that I had acquired woodworking skills from my dad and from working on boats and home repair. "Do you have any experience restoring antiques or frames?" he asked.

"My mother ran a ceramics studio," I replied, "and I picked up a lot of art skills watching her shape the ceramics and paint them in various finishes."

"Do you have a shop?" he asked.

"No," I said, "but I have a lot of the tools you need for this kind of work."

He looked me over for a moment. I realized that my résumé was a bit thin, but I hoped I made up for it with my obvious enthusiasm and the can-do air that I'd acquired in the Merchant Marine. He said he had a vacant basement that was quite a mess. "If you'd be willing to clean it up," he said, "perhaps you could set it up as a studio and work there. I have plenty of small repair jobs if you can do the work."

In a moment we were on our way downstairs. It wasn't nearly as bad as he'd made it sound, and I knew I could tackle it. Indeed, I was eager for the chance to throw myself into something that would involve using my hands and some good, old-fashioned, honest labor. We struck a deal on the spot, and I went home and used one of the templates from my past employment to draw up a simple lease agreement dated January 2000, titled "For the Restoration and Repair of Antiques and Picture Frames."

It took me a few days to bring all of my tools from my mother's home on Long Island and set up a modest restoration studio equipped with work lights and an exhaust fan. The whole arrangement felt like a situation orchestrated by heaven. Within a week the owner began bringing me jobs to do. As I passed each "test," the work became more challenging, and my confidence grew proportionately. I purchased some books on restoration and brought in the big book that my father had given me on the work of the great painter and sculptor Michelangelo, upon which I drew for inspiration as I restored carvings and ornate frames. As my little library grew and the jobs piled up, I watched my smooth executive's hands grow callused. I was thrilled that I was no longer aiding and abetting the mortgage industry by preparing appraisals to be used in foreclosing on people's homes.

About a month into my new occupation, the owner called me into his office and said that he was doing a major job at the home of a prominent film director. The work he'd brought me consisted of a pair of antique carvings from an old European church. Carefully unwrapping the carvings, swathed in pieces of old linen, he began to tell me their history. They looked like gargoyles of the sort displayed on churches to ward off evil.

As he shared with me his vision to restore the carvings, he

mused that they probably had not been worked on since the master sculptor created them centuries ago. One had simply lost its luster while acquiring layers of soot and candle wax. The other was a different matter altogether: in addition to being covered in layers of grime, its face had been so disfigured that the nose and part of one ear were missing.

The owner looked up to gauge my reaction. "What do you think?" he said. "Could you reconstruct the facial features of this carving? Don't say yes if you can't do it. If you do it, they must match, and the job has to look like Old World craftsmanship. My future with this client depends on that."

I surveyed the carvings. Even in their distressed state, they were beautiful, made from some kind of European hardwood that had darkened over the centuries to a deep brown patina. Looking within, I asked myself if I could do it, because I knew it would be a stretch. And I got back a yes.

"Yes," I said to the owner. "I believe I can restore this unknown master's church figure to near its original glory."

I gave him an estimate, he approved it, and I promised to give the job top priority, as I could see the concern in his expression. We shook hands on the deal. It was the first time we'd ever done that on a job, and he seemed to be emphasizing that he was trusting me with his reputation and with a valuable work of art. It was Friday, so I said I would begin the transformation process first thing on Monday. With some reverence I picked up the designer's treasures and transported them to my basement studio, placing them on a bed of burlap on my carpenter's worktable.

I stopped at the florist's on my way home and picked up some flowers for a date. I showered and shaved and then called my date to confirm. Her roommate answered and informed me that she had left town after receiving a last-minute invitation to go golfing. That hurt. I began moping around my apartment feeling sorry for myself, and then thought, *Hey, let me try to make the best of this.* I now had the night free, and I could get a head start on the challenging restoration project.

Besides, I couldn't blame the young lady for changing her plans without notice. Our last time out together I had told her that I'd quit my white-collar position with no new work lined up to, in essence, follow my bliss. The dream job I laid out for her must have sounded vague at best. I said that I had had some exposure to medicine as a medical corpsman in the Merchant Marine but that I had also been interested in spirituality, meditation, and tai chi. Now I wanted to follow my bliss, to pursue complementary and alternative healthcare. She looked at me indulgently before asking, "As a hobby, you mean?" That question should have been enough to make me see the writing on the wall. I pictured her out with some aspiring financial wizard, and I didn't expect to see her again.

So I hung up my dress shirt and put on my paint-splotched jeans and an old business shirt with frayed cuffs. I paused in my kitchen to collect the dozen salmon roses I had intended to present to my date. I didn't want to be reminded of my humiliation, and as I passed Memorial Sloan-Kettering Cancer Center, I handed the flowers to the surprised receptionist and asked him to give them to someone who might appreciate them.

By the time I got to my studio, it was nearing ten o'clock. I descended into the calm of my basement, and the smell of sawdust and furniture wax distracted me from my career challenges and the disappointment of a failed relationship. I pulled up my stool and unwrapped the old carvings, with no premeditated plan. I simply meditated on them for a good half hour, picking them up, turning them around, and seeking a solution. I sipped some coffee. It was going to be a long night, and once I got into a project, I seemed to lose track of time.

I needed some insight, some inspiration on how to begin the

procedure of reconstructing a nose and ear, something I'd never done before. As I glanced at my shelf, I spotted the book that my dad had brought back from Italy twenty years ago with shiny close-up photos of work by Michelangelo. I propped open the book and let my eyes take in the inspired genius. I tried to comprehend how this man had so profoundly captured human flesh in marble, making it come alive with a luminescence that belied the cold stone. That ability to defy nature had attracted commissions from the financial titans of his time, the Medici family, and even the Pope, who commissioned him to memorialize God's accomplishments on the ceiling of Rome's Sistine Chapel.

I drank in the fluid grace in the nose of perhaps the most famous statue in the world, his Florentine David. As I studied the sculpture of the young David, I recalled his story. Goliath, the champion of the Philistines, had been challenging the Israelites to send out a warrior to decide the outcome of a battle in single combat. Saul, the king of the Israelites, couldn't find anyone to fight the towering Goliath until an unlikely candidate, a teenage boy named David, stepped up and said he was not afraid. David approached the enemy with only his sling and five stones taken from a nearby stream. Encouraged and inspired by a noble cause, David went up against seemingly impossible odds. Aiming his primitive sling, he cast a small stone at a foe who had terrorized great warriors, and he brought Goliath crashing to his knees.

As I meditated on the photograph of the statue, I was moved by the complexity of Michelangelo's work. I tried to connect to some insight into the consciousness of the artist and the secret of his inspiration. What was it that enabled Michelangelo to do what no human had done before? He somehow captured a complex emotion in David's face: the boy doesn't exactly look fearful, yet he appears concerned, almost sad. He isn't taking the challenge lightly. And with that I read the humble words that the artist had left for those who sought to understand how he achieved his inspired work:

> . . . beauteous art, which, brought with us from heaven,
> will conquer nature; so divine a power . . .

With that enigmatic quotation resonating in my head, I sought to comprehend the consciousness of a man who deflected praise and offered it up to heaven. Like the inspired musical geniuses Mozart and Bach, he gave the credit for his inspiration to a divine Source. And with this emotion in my soul, I embarked in the shadow of the master with a tiny seed of faith that I could restore the art before me. So began the process of restoration on my first commission.

I put on my apron, set out my implements—the Navy surplus medical corpsman tools, the delicate files and old scalpels and natural sponges—and adjusted my overhead lights. I turned on the exhaust fan and opened the doors to Second Avenue to allow the cool air to ventilate the studio. Placing the carvings on their backs side by side, I tore off a piece of the old linen they'd been wrapped in and dampened it with nail polish remover. I used the acetone to strip away the grime and candle wax that had accumulated on the faces of the carvings over the years, and then I quickly dried them.

With the cleaned carvings before me, I could assess the extent of their damage and decided to begin by making a new nose for the defaced carving. I closely examined the face from all angles and imagined how the nose should look. Even though it wasn't a human figure, to the designer it was extremely valuable. Then I reached to the top of my bookshelf and pulled down a book I had come to rely on, *The Furniture Doctor* by George Grotz, with its easy-to-follow illustrations. I searched for a solution and soon found it in the concept of dowels used to join pieces together seamlessly.

I looked once more at the face of Michelangelo's *David*, and, like a diamond cutter about to split a priceless gemstone, I didn't move a muscle until I had conceived the new nose clearly in my mind. Without taking my eyes off the sculpture, I picked up my drill and carefully bored a slender pilot hole into the face to accommodate the post, exactly as I had seen oral surgeons do on a television program, inserting a titanium screw into the jawbone of a woman in preparation for anchoring a prosthetic tooth after a car accident had dislodged the natural one.

I could feel my perspiration building, and I wiped the sweat from my brow. Then I broke off a large hunk of artist's restoration putty, shaped a rough mass, gently anchored it to the screw, and allowed it to set. The technical aspect addressed, I moved on to the aesthetic part. I studied David's nose, the intricacies that formed the nostrils and the perfect symmetry of the whole, losing all concept of time. Before I knew it, the artist's putty had set, and I picked up my delicate curved rasp and began to shape first the bridge, then the nostrils, staring at the nose from the front and dropping my face to table level to gauge its length. Finally I rounded the tip of the nose.

I was flying by the seat of my pants, an untrained sculptor, as the shapely nose was released from the rough lump of putty. I was thankful, and my gratitude grew as I realized I was having fun again, maybe for the first time in years. The perfect nose that I saw in the mass of putty was set free, as if I were drawing on divine inspiration, and I carved away to create the vision of the nose in my mind's eye. Once the nose was fully formed, I sanded it smooth with fine emery paper. Then I heated a sewing needle to a glowing red and pressed it into the hardened putty, making random dots to mimic the wood grain in the sister sculpture.

Finally, I stained the gray putty of the nose to match the deep amber tone of the rest of the aged wood.

When that was done, I applied amber paste butcher wax to the pair and buffed each one perhaps a hundred times with rapid strokes, the friction melting the wax and allowing it to become transparent. As I polished away, each buff revealed more of the wood's lovely warmth, allowing it to regain its original radiance.

It was now about three in the morning, and I was hot from all the buffing. I released the carvings from the clamps holding them steady and propped them up against a chair whose legs I had been restoring earlier in the week. I grabbed my camera and took some photos to remember this job by. Just looking at the formerly disfigured carving, as the amber wax filled in the imperfections and allowed the new nose to blend seamlessly with the rest of the face, I couldn't discern where the break had been and where the new nose I had shaped began.

This was clearly the finest work I had ever done, and it seemed way better than I should have been able to produce based on my experience. I recalled the words of a woman I'd known named Marion Simons, who had graduated from the University of Virginia with a degree in architecture and was now on staff at Sotheby's. A native of Charleston, Marion possessed a grace and Old World charm beyond her years. She told me one day that it was a revered tradition in architecture and art that, after manifesting something from within you, you take a moment to feel gratitude for being blessed with the capacity to channel the inspiration of art.

Deciding to take her advice to heart, I sat up on my stool and looked at the carvings with a feeling of thankfulness in my heart. After a while, as I sat in that meditative state, I became aware that the sadness that had hung over me so heavily at the start of that night had evaporated. I realized that my restoration job might not have been a great accomplishment. It wasn't as if I had restored the face of a child with a congenital deformity. This was only an old, disfigured carving, but the warmth with which I had imbued the antique wood made it look natural and timeless. It didn't have the artificial tone that I had seen in the faces of some women I encountered strolling along the Upper East Side, who had had nose jobs and facial tucks.

My artist's eye could usually tell which noses had been surgically altered. God-given noses possess a natural balance, and the warm coloring from the natural circulation to the skin matches the coloring in the rest of the face. Whereas noses that have been surgically "enhanced" tend to look cold and taut, and their coloring can seem unnatural. These carvings before me emanated warmth, like things that God had made. And so, although it seemed a small thing, I felt about them a far greater sense of satisfaction than I ever had in closing a million-dollar real estate deal. I also believed that the joy I felt would last longer than my fleeting exhilaration at making a quick buck and then rushing out to buy myself a new trinket.

I continued to feel gratitude for the new nose and the natural warmth I had created, for even though my income had taken a serious downturn, I could now allow myself an entirely new kind of luxury—the luxury of dreaming. The thought occurred to me that, although God hadn't blessed me with the fast reading skills to get through med school, He had given me the artistic prowess to breathe new life into a broken sculpture. I hadn't experienced so much joy since I was a child. Without the burden of a daily job I loathed, I allowed my imagination free rein. In my mind's eye I saw the faces of children I had watched exiting the hospital nearby. And as I let my imagination fly, I dreamed . . . *Wouldn't it be great if doctors could restore these children seamlessly to blend the skin grafts and prosthetic ears and noses the way God had permitted me to shape wood, to make it breathe and appear alive?*

In essence, I wished they could do for suffering human beings what I had done for this disfigured carving. My boldness grew as my heart expanded in the joy of the moment. *Wouldn't it be amazing if I could shape and restore the faces of children with my hands the way my gift to sculpt allowed me to shape wood?*

As I held the sensation of that thought in my heart, a smile grew on my lips and I began to feel immense happiness and joy. I imagined that my joy was akin to what the children would feel if they could be healed, and their joy became my joy as I imagined them walking the streets unnoticed. I guessed that for many of them the greatest wish was to be *un*remarkable, to look so ordinary that nobody would give them a second glance.

And then it happened. Before my eyes, less than two feet away, a shape started to appear like little bits of iridescent sand forming into a solid mass. I was transfixed as the shape gradually took form, growing denser, until it resembled a freshwater pearl. This pearl of light rolled upon itself as if around an unseen center. And then it pulsed. It seemed as though a tiny chick were trying to break out of its shell with its beak. Suddenly, a ray of illumination shot straight up and down and to the left and right, forming a pair of axes. My heart began to beat very fast, yet I didn't blink. I couldn't have taken my eyes off what I was seeing if I had wanted to.

Then the pearl pulsed again and exploded, like a cloud in a lightning storm, the energy passing through my face and into my skull, searing the backs of my eyes with energetic lightning. My hair seemed to stand up on my scalp and the back of my neck, and then, *boom!* Everything went pitch black. There was not even a faint glow, nothing but complete darkness.

My heart was beating so fast that I could hear the blood pulsing in my ears and my heart beating in my chest. I sat perfectly still. I couldn't see. I was . . . blind! My first thought was simply *How did that happen?* I tried to stay rational. It must have been the acetone on the rags that I had used earlier that evening to remove the old wax. The label had a warning that it could be harmful and said to use it in a well-ventilated room. But I had opened the double doors to the street and turned on the powerful commercial exhaust fan in the back.

As I sat in silence, rationality waned and my anxiety quickly accelerated. *My God,* I thought. *I'm blind. I'm alone, I have few friends. Who will take care of me? Who would want to marry me? Why was I so stubborn? Why didn't I compromise? Why did I have to pursue my bliss? Couldn't I just forget the two-thousand-year-old wisdom found in the desert that had inspired me to bring forth what was in me? Stupid, stupid me!*

Minutes passed, and I grew more anxious and frightened. Who could I call? And then, at the height of my panic, I began to see what looked like the flickering of an old black-and-white TV. A snowy haze started to flicker before me, then blotches of light sparked in my periphery. Shadows of black and white gave way to wisps of color. And then, as mysteriously as it had vanished, my vision returned. I could make out the familiar confines of my studio, my books, my tools, the carvings in front of me. *My God, I'm not blind!*

Relief gave way to curiosity and wonder. *What had just happened to me?* I looked at the church carvings standing there, and a curious feeling overtook me. I recalled the article about the farmer in Egypt who had discovered the ancient vessels containing the lost secret teachings, and how he had hesitated to open them at first for fear that they might contain an evil genie. What if the sculptures that I had rubbed back to life had released some long-held negative energy? It sounded preposterous in a technological age, but I was still shaken from my experience and needed to do something to combat my admittedly irrational fears.

There was a church across the street next to the coffee shop

I frequented. I had never been in it, but an idea occurred to me. Taking off my apron, I put on my work jacket, grabbed a clean Portuguese natural sea sponge from my box of art supplies, and headed up and out. I had been at work so long that it was nearing sunrise; the streetlights were still on, and the traffic had slowed. I approached the front of the church, St. John's, wondering if I would be welcome there. I hadn't been in a church since I was a boy, when the priests had frightened me with their intimidating faces. Then I saw a small sign: THERE ARE NO STRANGERS—JUST FRIENDS WE HAVEN'T MET. I took that as a valid invitation and went to open the solid red center doors. Locked.

I went around to the smaller side door, where a wrought-iron gate with a chain and an open padlock dangling from it seemed to offer entry. Odd, I thought, if they were concerned about security, but maybe the cleaning crew had come in early and left the gate unlocked. I opened the gate and looked up the stone stairs. A small, round stained-glass window pictured a dove diving down from a brilliant blue sky, lit by a single bulb behind it. I bounded up the four steps, grabbed the handle, and tried again. This time the yellow oak door gave way. In my work shoes and paint-splattered pants, I might have looked like a homeless person, but I decided to chance it. The vestibule was perfectly quiet and still, as a church at five in the morning should be. Spotting what I came for—a small glass vessel mounted on the wall containing holy water—I reached in my coat pocket, removed the sea sponge, and dipped it in the pool. I drew it back and cupped it in my hand, fighting a childish fear that some priest would seize me by the ear. I skipped down the stairs and dashed back across the street and into my studio.

Laying the beautiful old church figures on their backs, I gave each of them a healthy dose of sacred medicine. I squeezed the holy water from the sponge right into their open mouths; the old, dried wood drank in the water completely. I felt a bit silly, but even if they held no negative energy, I would sleep easier now.

The next day I presented the sculptures to the designer, who was thrilled to be reunited with his treasures. He looked down at the two carvings before him and picked up one of them. A grin broke out on his face. "You did such a wonderful job," he said, "that I can't even see where the broken nose used to be."

Unknowingly, he had picked up the carving that had not been restored! I didn't have the heart to point out to the proud art expert that he was admiring the *unbroken* carving. As an after-thought, he glanced at the other carving and smiled approvingly. "I can barely tell which one was damaged," he said. I thanked him for his compliment and said it was a rewarding experience for me, too, to have the opportunity to work on the old sculp-tures and learn from the inspired master who had carved them so long ago.

Unbeknownst to me, that experience in my basement studio had been far more rewarding than I could possibly have imag-ined. On the morning that I climbed the stairs to the street, pass-ing beneath the hanging sign that read TRANSFORMING ORDINARY INTO EXTRAORDINARY, my life had been irrevocably transformed. I learned in the weeks that followed that something momen-tous had happened to me during the interval between evening and dawn of that January day. As my sculptor's hands had busied themselves, and my mind immersed itself in the meditative pro-cess of restoring the damaged nose of that old church carving, I had allowed myself the momentary luxury of imagining as a child does. My imagination took flight and soared. I had begun to think how wonderful it would be if I could use my gift to sculpt to restore the noses and faces of disfigured children, and how happy they would be. And as I had allowed myself to experience the joy they would feel if this were possible, their joy became my joy.

At that moment, my dream had climbed the stairs of my basement studio, had risen up through the morning sky, ascending to heaven, and had knocked on the door to the Unseen. And the Unseen had responded so overwhelmingly, so profoundly, that I was soon after witnessed by medical doctors to have realized the capacity to transform human tissue in a matter of minutes, which enabled me to actualize my dream of restoring people's limbs and facial features. Within a few years I had joined with a cross-disciplinary team of brave doctors, scientists, and theologians who were as eager as I to study, record, and educate the public about the profound potential of the mind-body-spirit connection to benefit health and healing, not only for the patient but also for the community. Among other things, they advised me to document the details of the events following my discovery and to record the events in my life that shaped my thinking up to that moment in my studio. In the following chapters I have set out to record for you the significant steps along the journey I followed to ignite the latent human potential to manifest physical change. In the tradition of other pioneers in all fields of exploration, I hope to create a map for others to follow. This is the Five Step path that is laid out in Part II.

Following the advice of my mentors, I will start at the beginning, when I thought with the limitless mind of a child.

Chapter 3

---

# CHILD'S PLAY

Genius is no more than childhood
recaptured at will.
—Charles Baudelaire

When I was nine years old, I had an experience that foreshadowed the transformation in my basement studio that I've just described. This childhood event was as profound in its own way, and it seemed to open doors of possibility—though they quickly slammed shut and remained that way until some thirty years later. Indeed, only in retrospect was I able to understand its significance in my personal evolution.

It was the summer of 1969, a time when all things seemed possible, when old ideas about the limits of human potential were being shattered in all fields of endeavor. And in the light of these emerging new truths, the hearts and minds of the children of my generation were unconsciously being instilled with the seeds of limitless potential and the possibility of achieving new realities. It was a moment in time when the inspired visions of two great leaders bore fruit. The prophecy of the country's youngest president, John F. Kennedy, was made manifest with the fulfillment of his promise of placing a man on the moon—an achievement that had seemed to many unimaginable just a few short years before. And with that first astronaut's small step on the surface of the moon, all of humanity for the first time in history seemed to march in unison, achieving a giant step forward.

Meanwhile, back on planet Earth, Dr. Martin Luther King's dream of equality and opportunity was building momentum. Who could have known that the televised march of a few hundred dedicated pioneers of the American civil rights movement over the Selma bridge just four years before would carry on for decades, continuing to shatter ignorance and manifest sweeping change, creating unprecedented opportunities in education and employment for all sexes, creeds, and colors? The watermen of the Mississippi delta will tell you that if you wish to gauge the magnitude of a vessel that has passed by, all you have to do is measure the size of the waves the vessel has left in its wake. By the evidence of the waves still being made some fifty years after King's ship passed through these waters, his stature is still growing.

But that summer I was just nine years old and didn't have the majestic intentions of a Kennedy or King; like most children, I thought with the mind of a child and wanted childish things. That summer was new terrain for me, a memorable time in my life, when I spent a few weeks away from my parents' supervision. Mom and Dad had embarked with a group of my father's coworkers on a well-deserved two-week journey through the major cities of Italy. My dad had been to Italy before he was married, when he served in the Navy aboard the USS *Newport News,* but this was my mother's first trip out of the United States. A woman with the heart of an artist, who operated a humble ceramics studio in the basement of her home, she was eager to nourish her soul and experience firsthand the legacies left by Michelangelo and

Da Vinci. Their inspired art reflected the majesty of the unseen spiritual realm so profoundly that centuries later it could still captivate a humanity besotted by transient technological achievements. The allure of those new trinkets, like the eight-track tape player in my father's car that was all the rage for a few years, sometimes fades into the realm of the obsolete as rapidly as it appears.

Along with my brother, Jake, age ten, and my sister, Cassie, age seven, I had resided all my life in New York City, where Dad worked. So the thought of spending two weeks in the country was infused with excitement and mystery. We would be with my dad's parents, Duke and Maude, at their summer cottage in Beach Lake, Pennsylvania, a sleepy rural town in the northeastern part of the state, near the Delaware Water Gap. That summer my brother and I sat on my grandmother's sofa and watched the moon landing on her ten-inch black-and-white television set, with aluminum foil wrapped around the rabbit-ear antennas in a low-tech effort to improve the reception. I was mesmerized, along with millions around the world, as a seemingly impossible technological achievement was made manifest. We were able to share even the thoughts going through Neil Armstrong's mind as he took that first step on the moon.

That sense of connecting with beings and events far removed in time or space was mirrored in more mundane events here on the ground. The small church Grandma attended in the summer was a half mile off the main road, through the woods that separated the crop farms from the cattle farms. Grandma and I had a ritual we would engage in whenever possible that we called "going deer counting." Just before dusk, she would pack up her three grandchildren and drive us down the unpaved country road that led to the little church in the woods. As we drove deeper into the forest and passed under the thick canopy formed by the old-growth trees, the sunlight would mysteriously vanish. Tilting my head to peer up, I could see the sun occasionally peek through the leaf cover, creating a kaleidoscope of shades. To my child's eyes it resembled multicolored stained-glass windows, as if some unseen architect had created a cathedral in the forest for the wild animals to enjoy. Grandma would bring the car to an almost imperceptible crawl, pausing momentarily at the entrance of each clearing formed by the freshly cut fields. She would tell us three "city kids" to be very quiet, to talk only in whispers as we watched for the animals to emerge from the forest to forage.

On the first day we set out to "go deer counting," I was quite impatient and questioned Grandma's promise that we would see "wild animals." "I don't see any animals," I kept repeating from the backseat. I was frankly suspicious of her claim that a whole world of wildlife shared the wooded land around our cottage. After all, who took care of these animals? At home in the city, we had two dogs, Beauregard and Rhea, and they needed all sorts of care—not just daily feeding and walking but also having their nails clipped, their fur brushed, frequent trips to the vet for shots of all sorts. So, I wanted to know, who took care of the animals of the fields?

"Just because you can't see them," Grandma would say, "doesn't mean they aren't there. Believe me, they're there all right, waiting for the safety of the sunset to enter the fields and feed on the bounty of corn scraps and crops that fell by the wayside as the tractors went about harvesting. Just be patient."

Cassie was too small to see over the door, and she seemed to look at me like a mirror, to share vicariously in what I was seeing as I peered out the windows. And then, sure enough, a herd of deer emerged from the edge of the woods, breaking into the clearing so fast that I couldn't count them all. They were crossing the dirt road before us and behind the car, jumping with great ease almost silently over the man-made stone walls and fences separating the fields. The next day we saw a parade of wild turkeys walking in single file, and then a fox that popped his head up, standing on his back legs as if he were watching us. Knowing such animals only from schoolbooks and TV, I was delighted to experience them on their home turf.

That summer was very healing, as if my body had been craving fresh air and water. And it was a mental break from school as well, especially for a child who found certain subjects, like geometry, easy but had difficulty with grammar and spelling. It frustrated me that the other children could read with such ease, and it remained a mystery both to me and to my parents until the time I was diagnosed as having attention deficit disorder. So the summer was a time to relax and play, a time to forget schoolwork and chores.

As I said, I thought like a child, and I had childish desires. My older brother was already a foot taller than I was, and he was also a whiz at math and excelled at sports. Jake was a hard act to follow. What's worse, because I was the younger brother, it seemed that all the things I owned—my pants and shirts, winter boots, toys, and bicycle—were well-worn hand-me-downs that he had outgrown. I didn't understand why I always got his castoffs. To my parents, naturally, it made perfect sense, like eating all my vegetables with dinner. But, understandably, my early childhood was preoccupied with a yearning to have something new and unused, something of my own.

One day during the spring before my parents went to Italy, Dad and I were sent on an errand. Dad drove us to a famous Jewish bakery on Emmons Avenue in Brooklyn that made unbelievably tasty rye bread my mother loved. When we arrived, my father kept driving past the bakery in search of a parking spot. On our way back to the bakery, my little legs moved quickly to keep up with my dad's six-foot, four-inch frame. Something caught my eye from the window of a shop. There she was calling to me, like she was waiting for me, a brilliant iridescent blue Schwinn Sting-Ray bicycle with a banana seat. I wanted that bike more than anything else in the world; it cost close to two hundred dollars, and from that day I began to dream about having that bike.

After the first day deer counting, while I was still digesting the mystery of where the wild animals disappeared to during the day, Grandma announced we were going on another outing. She would be taking us to the church in the woods, which was having a fair to raise money for repairs. She had already baked a few loaves of Irish soda bread in cast-iron pans that would be sold along with the other donated items from members of the community who had sifted through their attics and garages.

So early in the afternoon, with warm bread loaves in the front seat, Grandma drove Jake and me to the church, although as hard as I looked, those darn deer wouldn't show themselves. Armed with the dollar she had given each of us to spend at the fair, Jake and I set out exploring the tables full of secondhand tools, toasters, and other castoffs. But I had enough secondhand things. And then came the good stuff: Grandma's Irish soda bread next to some chocolate cakes and lemon cupcakes that smelled awfully good. I was tempted to get one of those cupcakes, but knowing I could always have a treat when I got home, I went on exploring with Jake. Jake picked up a toy from a table, a wooden paddle with a red rubber ball attached to it by a long rubber band. He started to flip his wrist and soon mastered bouncing the ball rapidly in the center of the paddle. I was instantly jealous, as racket games were yet more things I couldn't do. I looked at the other toys and some used Matchbox cars, but I wasn't ready to part with my only dollar just yet, and certainly not for some other kid's used toys. I was waiting for something really good. While Jake played with the paddle, I wandered off to see what I could find. At the edge of the picnic ground behind the church, I saw a table with a lot of people crowded around chatting excitedly, laughing and clapping. Above the table was a hand-painted sign that read WHEEL OF CHANCE.

I worked my way up to the table, getting some raised eyebrows from the adults, none of whom I recognized from church. The wheel had ten numbers on it, and in front of it was a sheet of white vinyl with numbered boxes into which people were putting dollar bills. I did recognize the man spinning the wheel, an usher from the church named Jim. Jim knew my grandmother, and last Sunday when he had shoved a basket on a stick with felt lining in it in front of me and my brother, we'd each put in a quarter that Grandma had given us. But this wasn't church. I spoke up. "How does it work?" I asked. "What do you do? How do you win?"

For a second there was complete silence, then some guy sitting on a milk crate flipping a Zippo lighter, with too much grease in his silver-and-red-colored hair, laughed at me. I didn't like that, but I decided I would ignore him. I looked back at Jim, who looked at me kind of funny too. "Well, son," he said, "you guess the numbers that are going to come up on the Wheel of Chance and you put your money down. When you win, you get five times your money back!"

I couldn't believe what I was hearing. Wow, this was great! Grandma had never told me about this game. Here was the solution to my desire to get that iridescent blue bicycle with the gear shifter before some rich kid's dad snapped it up. I was so excited. I closed my eyes for a second and could see myself returning to that bicycle store with my dad, walking in and handing the money to the clerk as he lifted that beautiful bike out of the window. I could feel my hands on the rubber grips on the handlebars as I swung my leg over the seat and rode that bike right out of the shop, pedaling really fast—not like on the one-speed, little-kid, hand-me-down bike from my brother. As I daydreamed, I could feel the wind blowing in my face, riding so fast I had to squint to keep it out of my eyes. Boy, was I having fun!

Jim's authoritative voice pulled me out of my reverie. "Do you want to play?" I believed that I could trust Jim with my dollar, which at that moment represented my entire net worth. So I took the dollar out of the zippered pocket in my Cub Scout cargo pants and held it up to him, standing on my tippy-toes because the table was too high for me to reach. Jim bent down and asked me if that was my only dollar. I nodded yes.

The adults were grumbling, like the kids did in school when you asked a question that was holding things up. Someone from the crowd said, "Come on! Let's get on with the game." When Jim asked me if I was sure I wanted to bet it, I answered "*yes!*" so loud that a few people laughed.

"Okay, now tell me the number," Jim said.

"Seven, nine, five, three, one!" I said without thinking.

"No, son," he said, "just one at a time!"

So I said "Seven" and handed him the dollar bill, which he placed in the box on the table marked "7."

He spun the wheel, and 7 won.

The man standing on my left clapped me on the shoulder. "Hey, what do you know?" he said. "Beginner's luck!" I was excited but not surprised, and I kept my mind on the numbers I had recited. Before Jim was ready to spin again, I asked him to put the five dollars I had won on number 9. "Are you sure?" he said. I was. What was not to be sure of? This was easy. Jim spun the wheel again, and I felt a sense of exhilaration in my heart as 9 came up.

A couple of people applauded, and I quietly asked Jim to put my winnings onto the space for number 5. "All of it?" he asked. "Why don't you hang on to some of it?" Why, I wondered, was Jim working against me? Didn't he know I was on a mission to win enough money for my new bike—before my brother the math whiz got bored with his paddle game and found me at this game and won everything?

"All of it," I said. One of the older men called out gleefully, "Let it ride!"

Jim moved the money over, sighed loudly, and gave the wheel another spin. "Five's the winner!" he shouted.

I had no doubt. I believed I would win, and I did. Jim looked shocked, though, and he took his time counting out my winnings before handing the stack of bills down to me. The crowd was really buzzing now, as with each spin I got closer to realizing my dream of riding that bicycle. I took the money and without hesitating handed it back to Jim. I told him to put it on number 3— my favorite number.

"Slow down, young fella," Jim said sharply. He was looking over my head into the crowd waving at someone. "You might not win the next game. That's a lot of money. You don't want to lose it all!"

But there was no doubt in my mind that I would win. For me it was child's play. Despite his protestations, I knew I had the winning number. "Number three," I said.

This time a few people standing next to me placed bills on number 3 as well. Jim took a moment separating the bills into separate piles, then did something different. He reached all the way to the top of the wheel and gave it a violent spin. And instead of going around two or three times, like in the first three spins, it rotated almost five times, so fast that the numbers blurred. By now, hearing the shouts and laughter, people were leaving nearby tables to see what all the excitement was about. When the wheel came to rest on number 3, a shout like an explosion went up from the small crowd that had grown behind me. Finally, not happy at all, Jim handed me a pile of bills, paid off the other two winners, then closed his empty cashbox. "Sorry, folks, that's enough," he said. "The boy broke the bank. Game's over."

I took the bills he handed me and put them in various pockets of my shorts. I was glad I'd worn my Cub Scout shorts, because they had lots of pockets with zippers. I didn't have to count the money; I was certain I had enough to buy that bicycle. The dream I'd held in my heart of that new bike was within my grasp. I could feel the eyes of the others on me, and not all of them were friendly. "Craziest thing I ever saw," one of them said.

As I was tucking the last of the dollars into my leg pocket, a dollar bill fell to the grass near my right sneaker. I bent down to pick it up. That's when someone grabbed me from behind. I felt two fingers grasp my right earlobe so hard it hurt! At once I was being propelled through the crowd by a powerful force, with all the adults looking on. It was Grandma. Her fingers continued to pinch my ear and wouldn't let go. There were guffaws from some of the men still at the table, but Grandma was dead serious. Her face was stern, and I'd never seen her so angry before. What had I done wrong?

"Come with me, young man!"

She walked me to the dirt parking lot beside the church. There, between two cars, stood the pastor, who had already heard about the closing of the one table that held the most potential to raise enough money to pay for the repairs to the church. Away from the sounds of the crowd, Grandma finally let go of my ear. "What do you think you're going to do with all that money, young man?"

"Buy a new brand-new bike!" I said. I was still so excited about that bike, and excited to tell Grandma, that I hadn't put all the pieces together yet.

"No," she said, "you're not."

"But I know the kind I want. A Schwinn Sting-Ray! There's one in the store near where we live."

"You're going to give all that money back."

"But it's my money!" I said, incredulous. "I won it! Ask Jim."

"That money's not for you to keep," she said. "Now you take all those dollar bills out of your pockets and your socks and wherever else you've stuffed them and put them up here right now."

With that she smacked her palm down on the trunk of a car.

"All of them?" I asked.

"Every bill."

"I *have* to?"

"Yes. You have to."

I loved Grandma Maude, but I didn't understand. Slowly, I emptied all my pockets. I put the money on the trunk of the car the priest was standing next to. He was looking from side to side, and he seemed uncomfortable. It took a while; the money was all in fives and ones. Finally, I came to the last dollar bill, the one dollar that Grandma had given me to spend any way I wanted to. So I knew at least that one dollar was mine to keep. I showed it to Grandma Maude and said, "My dollar," and started to put it back in my pocket. She stopped me.

"That too."

"But, Grandma, you gave me a dollar to spend."

"You spent it," she said. Grandma collected the bills, folded them neatly, and handed the money to the pastor, looking terribly embarrassed. "I'm so sorry for the trouble, Father," she said.

The priest waved his hand. "Are you sure the boy couldn't keep just—"

She interrupted him. "Like you said, Father, the proceeds from today are for upkeep and repairs, and that is where this money is going. All of it!"

Then she turned to me. "Now apologize to the pastor."

My face turned red. I don't even remember what I said, but I couldn't believe that I had to apologize for something I didn't understand. The pastor took the last dollar bill. He was a big man, almost as tall as my dad, and, as he did, he leaned down closer to my face. He didn't seem angry at all. "So," he said, "how did you do it, son?"

"Do what?"

"Know what numbers to choose."

"I just knew."

"*How* did you know? What was your secret?"

I couldn't explain it. "I just knew."

Grandma told me to wait in the car while she went on apologizing some more. I sat in the front passenger seat, and she came over and gave me the head shake and the you're-a-naughty-boy look. "Sit still and don't move," she said. "I'm going to find your brother." A few minutes later she returned with Jake, who was looking a bit confused about the hasty departure. On the ride home, Grandma was uncharacteristically silent. In the backseat Jake played with the paddle and rubber ball he had purchased with his dollar. I sat there with my arms folded and my lower lip stuck out in a serious pout. Grandma looked over and caught my unmistakable body language. "Joey," she said as compassionately as she could, "I know you're upset, and I know you don't understand all this."

She looked back at the road, then she added, "There's a saying that I love, and it goes like this. 'When I was a child, I spoke as a child, I understood as a child, I thought as a child. But, when I became a man, I put away the things of a child.'" After that, she never spoke again about the church fair or the Wheel of Chance.

That summer was full of wonderful mysteries that I couldn't fully comprehend. I learned that being open to knowing in a way other than using our five senses was frowned upon at a minimum. And if one did act on that knowing, one could end up receiving physical pain, intense censure, and humiliation. So I learned to suppress the experience that I'd had standing near the wheel and subconsciously altered my behavior to block out the knowing so as not to anger adults in the future.

# Chapter 4

---

# IN THE FOOTSTEPS OF GIANTS

Q: How is consciousness transformed?
A: Either by trials themselves or by
   illuminating revelations. Trials and
   revelations are what it is all about.
                          —Joseph Campbell,
                            *The Power of Myth*

I can vividly recall my parents' return from Italy that summer. In those two short weeks I had experienced intense excitement and revelation and crushing disappointment. At the same time as I was experiencing the mystical wonders of nature, I had held my childhood dream of getting that blue bicycle within my grasp, only to have it yanked away without an explanation that I could comprehend. So on the day my parents came to collect us, it was comforting to be reunited with them and be back in their world. Dad and Mom spent the afternoon regaling my dad's parents with details of their trip, from throwing pennies in the Trevi Fountain in Rome to seeing Michelangelo's statue of David in Florence. Dad had brought back an alabaster replica of the *David* that was about sixteen inches tall, and he told us children the story of how a young David had prevailed against the giant warrior Goliath because he had faith that he could destroy the bigger man. Still a small kid, I liked the idea of the diminutive but noble David overcoming the hulking giant. As the years passed, I spent many hours studying that statue, the most beautiful and perhaps only piece of art I remember from our home.

My dad didn't have much time for focus on art because he had to earn his living as a firefighter. The only time I actually saw him putting out a fire, a huge blaze at a restaurant near Sheepshead Bay in Brooklyn, I was scared to death for him. But he loomed as a larger-than-life hero whom I looked up to. And although it was true that my dad was a fireman by day, every night he had another identity as one of the most recognized cowboys in the world. The rugged looks that he had inherited from his parents, the face and build of a frontiersman or Wild West cowboy, embodied a maverick quality that many people in America, Europe, and the Far East secretly identified with. And it was a truth that the Mad Men—the men and women who worked in the advertising industry on Madison Avenue—hadn't failed to recognize either. In the late 1950s they set out to cast men to portray the iconic cowboy whom they styled the Marlboro Man.

My dad's first firehouse happened to be on the Upper East Side, in the same neighborhood as the ad agencies, and the admen who were always searching for rugged-looking guys for their print ads and TV commercials spotted Jack Farrell on the street. One of the ad execs gave my dad the name of an agent and encouraged him to make a visit. Within weeks my dad was sitting for the master illustrator Gustav Rehberger, who had been engaged by the company to create a series of Marlboro Man campaigns. In 1959 Gustav portrayed my dad with a light tan Stetson cowboy hat and denim jacket, throwing a saddle on a big horse. The original artwork for that iconic ad was later donated by Rehberger's widow to the Smithsonian Institution, where it remains in the permanent collection of Americana. That full-page ad featuring my dad as the famous cowboy ran in *Life* magazine and other periodicals circulated around the world. So as a result of that chance encounter on the streets of Manhattan, Dad landed a second job to supplement his firefighter salary beyond his wildest imagination. The ad agency and the company liked my dad so much that they also hired him to portray other cowboys in ads for products like Kellogg's cornflakes. From print Dad gradually moved up to television, culminating in the Marlboro Man commercials, and he even appeared on giant billboards throughout America.

Like families who say grace before meals in gratitude for the food on their plates, each evening the Farrells observed a strange way of expressing thanks. At 4:59, just before the news came on every evening, my mother would turn on the television, and we would watch in awe as my dad appeared on the screen, sitting on an Appaloosa stallion on a hillside in Flagstaff, Arizona. As the camera came in on a tight one-shot, Dad would turn and look into the lens, strike a match, and cup the flame with his hand to light a Marlboro cigarette. And then the camera would cut away, and Dad would race that horse down the hill and rope a steer. When the ad was over, the evening news would come on. Then my mother would clap her hands Amen!, turn off the TV, and announce that it was time to eat.

One day after she turned off the TV, I asked, "Why do we always do that, Mom?"

"Because," she said, "each time your dad rides that horse down the hill, he receives a residual, a payment for being in the ad. And one day we'll buy a new home and move out of the city. So if your dad keeps riding that horse down that hill and doesn't fall off, we'll have enough money to buy that home." With each viewing, she knew she was one step closer to achieving her dream—buying a house in the suburbs, with a big yard where her kids could play and the dogs could run.

As I reviewed the experience over the summer of my tenth year, what stood out was the realization that my dad routinely risked his life for other fathers, mothers, and children, people who were total strangers. The image of him in his firefighting gear, striding along that roof in Brooklyn amid the flames, merged with my memory of the astronauts I had watched walking on the moon in their space suits. The astronauts risked their lives to advance human knowledge and widen the world's horizons, but my dad risked his life to help other people on a daily basis, and that made him as big a hero in my eyes. Years later I would read Joseph Campbell's brilliant elucidation of the Hero's Journey, the archetypal path followed by all seekers, which he extracted from the world's varied mythological traditions, in which it appears in essentially the same form.

As Campbell explained it, the Hero's Journey is primarily a voyage of discovery to the center of yourself, to wholeness and understanding. It involves answering an inner call, breaking away from your familiar environment or family, and forging a new identity through a series of trials and adventures. Along the way, the hero—female or male—gets help from guides and mentors. If the hero survives the challenges of the journey, he or she may receive a great gift and must then decide whether to return to the world to offer the gift to humanity. This archetypal pattern profoundly influenced George Lucas, who based his Star Wars movies on it. In an interview, Campbell was asked about the deeds the hero performs along the way. "So in all of these cultures, whatever the local costume the hero might be wearing, what is the deed?"

"Well, there are two types of deed," Campbell answered. "One is the physical deed in which the hero performs a courageous act in battle or saves a life. The other kind is the spiritual deed, in which the hero learns to experience the supernormal range of human spiritual life and then comes back with a message."

At the age of nine, of course, I had no understanding of such profound patterns. I wasn't even sure what motivated people like the astronauts, my dad, or David in the Bible to risk their own lives to help other people. I was still in the foothills of my own journey and looking for guides and mentors without even knowing it. All I knew was that I felt excited by the message that we as a species have the potential to do great things. And by my watching and meditating on the "footsteps of the giants" that had captured my attention that summer, my consciousness was permanently altered.

A few years later, after my family had moved to our new home on Long Island and I started junior high school, I felt like I had arrived on a new frontier of my own. As a former city kid, I found many lessons to learn, including the importance of compassion and trusting your inner guidance. That lesson represented the next step in realizing my potential to manifest change. I went from being a spectator to taking the first small action to help another, a small action that altered the course of my life.

Chapter 5

# LESSONS FROM THE HEART

That one thing is compassion. This is
the theme that James Joyce takes over
and develops in *Ulysses*—the awakening
of his hero, Stephen Dedalus, to man-
hood through a shared compassion
with Leopold Bloom.

   —Joseph Campbell,
    *The Power of Myth*

It is the quality of our work that will
please God and not the quantity.

   —Mohandas Gandhi

The lessons we learn from life become deeply ingrained in each of
us and are remembered longer than the lessons we learn in school.
And the lessons you learn from your heart go a lot deeper than
the ones you learn with your mind. The crucial lesson I learned
during my early years was that the profound power and guidance

available to us from our hearts has the potential to remove the many obstacles and ignorance that plague modern-day humanity.

When we moved from the city to the suburbs, I felt like I had entered a new stage of my personal journey, one in which the lessons became more challenging. In buying a new home in Bayport, my parents were also facing new challenges, reaching beyond their station and beyond their means. If not for my dad's good fortune in being selected to appear in those ads and TV commercials, they might never have been able to make the transition. As it was, the prices of the new homes in the Bayport area were several times greater than what we would receive for the small house we planned to sell. The neighborhood that my parents chose was inhabited mainly by affluent professional people, and even with Dad's two jobs it was a real stretch. So he had sat down with the rugged Norwegian builder whose homes were in such demand that he couldn't build them fast enough and engaged in a little horse trading. Dad explained that he could do a lot of the finish work himself, the wood trim, carpentry, and painting—precisely the kind of labor that was most time-consuming, requiring a good eye and steady brush, and would be costly to subcontract. With his sons' help he could also do most of the landscaping and cut even more off the purchase price.

The builder could have passed for one of the frontiersmen who appeared in the Marlboro ads if not for his blond hair and pipe, so I think he and my dad felt pretty comfortable with each other. Shortly after he and Dad started talking, we heard the familiar deep, guttural laughs of working men, accompanied by a few backslaps to confirm that the two had conceived an imaginary bridge they could walk across, based on shared trust and a handshake, to make my mother's dream a reality.

Having grown up in a city where the children played ball on the streets and racket sports against concrete walls, I had no reference point for the landscape of the South Shore of Long Island. In the sleepy seaside town of Bayport, I would need to develop a whole new set of skills. I was just ten when we started house shopping out there, and, as I looked around the neighborhood, I didn't see any basketball courts or walls for playing paddleball; instead I saw tennis courts faux-painted the color of green grass and marinas with sailboats so abundant they looked like cars choking the parking lot at the new JC Penney mall. I wasn't sure how I was going to fit in, because I had no exposure to tennis, and I certainly hadn't ever been on a sailboat.

But when we moved out there, I made friends with a couple of the local kids. Our neighbors the Opinantes had two sons, Gary and Bill, both about my age, very bright and possessed of a dry sense of humor, perhaps acquired from their dignified Scottish mother, Betty. We bonded over the summer, and I learned that Bill was a sailor who had already won trophies in races called regattas. One afternoon as he was waxing the hull of his blue fiberglass sailboat in preparation for a race, he generously explained the basics of sailing and identified the parts of the boat. I met another boy named Bobby, who taught me how to surf-cast for the large sea trout and bluefish that migrated past our homes each year. So by the time school opened and I entered junior high at Bayport High School, I wasn't flying solo. I was starting to fit in again, but I became aware that the process of assimilation wasn't so easy for everyone else.

At the start of my second year of high school, my friends and I were eating our lunch when I saw a new kid stroll in. I watched him carry his food tray into the midst of the cafeteria looking for a place to park. At first I think I was just kind of amused at the spectacle. I heard some kid say, "Look at this new refugee! Oh, my God, fresh meat." I had been spared that experience. Tucking right into wing formation behind two of my neighbors, I'd slid into their table as nonchalantly as possible, not even checking the periphery for fear of catching the hostile looks that I knew would be lurking in all directions. But this poor kid headed straight toward a table full of jocks. What was he thinking? Those guys all had their school jackets emblazoned with varsity letters, establishing them as big men on campus, while the new kid looked more like a "math-lete" than an athlete. As expected, they brushed him off without even breaking their frenetic conversation. It was amazing how they could do it with just body language.

Next he walked up to a table that was full of cool girls, equally out of his league. They were school royalty, and unless your dad was the senior partner of a law firm or you had a varsity letter on your school jacket, you didn't even appear on their radar. They giggled at first at the breach in social etiquette, then cast stone-cold gazes at him. He stopped dead in his tracks, as if he had walked into some invisible force field. Next to the cool girls was the tough guys' table. The kid didn't even break stride. He put his head down and kept walking as one tough kid lobbed an empty milk carton to smack the back of his head; fortunately for the kid, it missed by a hair and skidded to a stop under a table. By now I was starting to feel kind of sorry for the guy. There was nowhere for him to sit, and my heart went out to him. He looked like one of those albatrosses at sea that fly for days searching for a place to land.

I looked away, though, willfully turning a blind eye. When I looked up again, he was still floundering, his eyes sweeping the room in near panic mode. I thought, *No way, not my responsibility,* and turned back to my friends. Then I looked a third time, and I realized I could no longer ignore the situation. My mind wasn't directing me, because it wasn't an intelligent decision. I knew it could backfire and diminish my security among my own group. I was still pretty new there myself, so it wasn't really up to me to extend an invitation. But I couldn't help myself. Without thinking, I casually slid a chair at the end of our table toward him with my foot. The slight gesture caught his eye, and I gave a nod in the direction of the seat. Even behind his thick glasses, the kid's eyes seemed to grow larger. I knew my buddies were going to rag on me, but, like I said, I wasn't thinking about that. I was just acting from a sort of silent conscience.

With the chair extended in his direction, the kid covered the fifteen feet of open space and dove into it, barely breathing lest the invite be rescinded. The guys at my table gave me some odd looks, but I just raised a shoulder and shrugged, and they didn't do anything beyond giving me that initial gaze of censure. I guess they figured it wasn't worth busting my chops about. The next day, like clockwork, the kid came over to our lunch table and stood there, like we had now inherited the problem, so I gave in and nodded to a chair. He sat there in silence, pretending not to listen to our conversation, so I finally turned to him and asked his name, where he was from, and where he was living now. He opened up to me, and, after we spoke, I turned to the group and said, "Hey, guys, this is Tim Knopf. Tim's from Pennsylvania, and he lives down on Newport Street."

Nods all around, no big deal, welcome to the club.

As Gandhi said, in matters of conscience, the law of the majority has no place. Most of the time we ignore our inner voices, because we don't logically see how we are helped by helping someone else. But the spiritual laws of the universe don't act two-dimensionally or in straight lines; they work in ways that are not so clear on the surface. These decisions don't always add up logically, yet, by listening to the inner voice, we may benefit in ways that we could never have imagined. As I have read more and shared stories with other seekers on the path, I have learned the principle espoused long ago by the Native Americans that what we do to the web—the interlocking circles of earth and human-ity—we do to ourselves. This concept is similar to the Eastern understanding of karma, a universal system of cosmic justice that evaluates your actions in a way akin to Newton's famous third law of motion: every action has an equal and opposite reaction. Maybe the simplest version of this principle, which proves more truthful to me each day, is that what you sow, you will reap.

I did reap a few unexpected results from my spontaneous reaching out to Tim that day. In time we became good friends, and I discovered that he was a talented tennis player—his dad had been a state college champion in Pennsylvania. At his father's suggestion, Tim helped me develop my tennis skills enough to make the school team. He was also generous in tutoring me informally for my chemistry exams, explaining concepts like the periodic table in ways that helped me boost my science test scores. But, as I said earlier, the real benefit of helping others lies not in any material rewards but in how such actions aid our inner growth.

Indeed, the value of compassion was brought home to me in a far more compelling way some years later, after I had had my transformative experience with those church carvings in my basement studio at the dawn of the new millennium. I knew I had been changed that night, I just wasn't sure how. Yet, within a matter of days, several people reported spontaneous healings in my presence. I wasn't trying to do anything, I wasn't putting my hands on anyone, but they were reporting healing from serious injuries while I was in their proximity. Some people might find that exciting and empowering, but I found it rather embarrassing.

One particularly disconcerting incident occurred at a dinner party while I was seated next to a man whose hand had been disabled. A childhood trauma had resulted in the loss of the use of his pinkie and ring finger. As I was engaged in conversation with a woman on the other side of me, I noticed this man's hand hovering around my bread dish. I figured he'd just mistakenly assumed it was his dish, but then I saw that his hand was trembling. He suddenly blurted out, "Oh, my God! I can feel my ring finger!"

I turned to look at him, more annoyed than anything else by his bizarre outburst. "You healed me!" he almost shouted. "I haven't been able to close my hand since I was a child. You're a healer!"

Because I had grown up in a conservative, working-class family, and then spent four years in a military college, my conscious mind instinctively rebelled against the label of "healer." Apparently, I had already forgotten that I had expressed a dream to perform just such acts only weeks before! I told him to calm down and not say things like that.

Several similar incidents occurred in the days that followed, and word got around. As a result, a man named Ted, who owned a mapmaking company in a midtown Manhattan building, offered to lease me a vacant office where I could meet with people who wanted to experience the work. A few days later, Ted and I were visiting my friend Beatta on Long Island, and as we sat on the beach, I was meditating with eyes half-open, in the dunes, protected from the wind. All of a sudden a Dalmatian came hobbling over to me, sat in my lap, and extended his paw. My heart went out to this injured creature, because I'd always loved animals and had grown up with two dogs. When I instinctively reached my hand toward the dog's swollen joint, I saw the swelling go down, and his leg, which had been bent and crippled moments before, straightened out. The dog started licking me all over, which got Ted laughing. The dog's owner, some distance down the beach, started calling him and seemed annoyed that he didn't run back. When the owner finally came over to me, his dog started running around in circles, acting quite thrilled with his restored mobility. The astonished owner observed the dog's behavior for a few moments, then asked, "How did you do that?"

At which point Ted interjected, "J.P. can heal people—and apparently now animals!"

The owner told us that a car had hit his dog some days before, but that the vet wanted six hundred dollars to treat the injury. "I'm just a working guy," he said, "and that was more than I could pay. I figured he'd get better on his own in time."

He looked bemused as the dog romped in the sand, showing no signs of his injury. "But it's odd," the man said, "because my dog never goes up to strangers."

After these and other incidents, I was increasingly contacted by people seeking relief from seemingly intractable health issues for themselves or loved ones. I never knew what to expect, so I had to keep my heart open to whatever might be required of me.

In the spring of 2002, I received a phone call from a woman named Louise regarding her husband, who was very ill. "Gene has a growing brain tumor," she said. "He has been diagnosed by the chief of neuro-oncology at the National Cancer Institute's Center for Cancer Research with a high-grade glioma. The doctors have added that it is inoperable." High-grade (or Grade IV) gliomas are cancers that originate in the brain, as opposed to those that develop elsewhere in the body and then spread, or metastasize, to the brain. (This is the very type of cancer that afflicted Senator Ted Kennedy and led to his death in 2009.) Further, during a radiation session, Gene had developed hemiparesis (weakness on one side of the body) and was now in a wheelchair.

I could hear the anguish in Louise's voice. "Have you ever worked with anything like this?" she asked.

I said that I hadn't and asked for more details. "This is my concern, Mr. Farrell," she said. "He has a large brain tumor that is growing, and he's in terrible pain. He's become habituated to the pain medication, and it just isn't relieving his suffering any longer. Do you think you can help his pain?"

I asked where they were located, and she said they were in Arlington, Virginia. Before his illness, Gene had worked at *The Washington Post*.

"I believe the brain tumor can be significantly reduced in size," I said.

"Do you think you can ease his pain?" she asked again.

I repeated that I thought the tumor could be reduced. It was as if she hadn't understood what I was saying. "But can you help his pain?" she said.

"I think when the tumor is reduced," I said at last, "this will eliminate the pain."

"Well, then," she said, "I'm going to bring him to you. When can I come?" Louise asked if my office was accessible by wheelchair, and I assured her that wouldn't be a problem.

Several days later, Louise wheeled her husband into my office and handed me his medical records. Gene's head was drooping onto his shoulder. Although he couldn't speak, he was fully conscious, and I could sense the pain he must have been experiencing. "I'm very upset," Louise said. "My husband is in terrible pain. He's only been given a couple of weeks to live. But if you can help ease his pain, I'd be terribly grateful."

The chart was dated April 12, 2002, and bore the heading of the National Cancer Institute's multidisciplinary brain tumor clinic. "I'm not a doctor," I said, examining the chart, "but thank you for this." The medical report identified the patient as "a fifty-seven-year-old right-handed Caucasian male with a right parietal glioblastoma multiforme." It stated further that "during radiation, patient had an acute left-sided hemiparesis requiring wheelchair at home." The physician's impression was that the tumor showed "increased enhancement and increased edema compared to prior scans," meaning that it was growing and swelling. "Based on the location of the patient's tumor," the chart stated, "he is not felt to be a surgical candidate."

What that meant, in cold, clinical language, was that the tumor was inoperable, and so there was nothing more they could do for Gene. Again Louise asked me if I could do anything about her husband's pain. "I believe," I said, "that his tumor can be significantly reduced in size."

"How much is this going to cost?" she asked. "Because the medical bills are killing me."

"Oh," I said, "there's no charge. All I ask is that when you take him back to Arlington for a follow-up exam, you send me a copy of the new MRI results."

She filled out a consent form and held the clipboard under his hand so Gene could scrawl his initials, which he was able to do unsteadily. Louise agreed that she would send me a copy of any medical reports or MRIs they received after returning home. With that, I asked Louise to help me get her husband onto my table, then asked her to make herself comfortable in the waiting room.

I allowed myself to create a state of empathy, of union with this man, who was so clearly suffering. (This state of empathy is beautifully conveyed in the film *Resurrection,* starring Ellen Burstyn. A detailed account of my own process of manifesting physical change appears in Chapter 15 of this book.) As soon as I connected myself to the Divine, the Source of all energy, I began to feel heat emanating from the right side of Gene's head. It was as if I had placed my hand near the open door of a pizza oven. At one point, as I held my hand five or six inches from Gene's head, over his right parietal lobe, I felt something like little shocks entering my palm. His head started quivering, wobbling slightly from side to side, and I could still feel heat coming from his right cerebral hemisphere. At the same time, I felt perspiration trickling down inside my shirtsleeves and collar as I began to warm up.

My brother, Jake, an engineer who studied thermodynamics—the science of energy conversion between heat and mechanical work—had explained to me that matter is made up of energy. When you transmute matter in any way, he said, you inevitably release energy in the form of heat. I sensed that, during the time I was working on Gene, the mass in his brain was somehow being transmuted into energy, generating heat from the area where the tumor was located. In any event, it felt like a lot of work to me. When I was done, after thirty minutes, I was exhausted. I had barely moved on my swivel stool during that time, but I was drenched in sweat. I got up and walked to the waiting room to invite Louise in.

"How did it go?" she asked. "Do you think you helped him?"

Given the vast release of energy I had experienced, I told her honestly what I thought. "I believe the tumor in his head has shrunk substantially," I said.

Louise looked at me. "Well," she said, "we will have to see about that." Then she looked closely at her husband. "He does look relaxed, though," she said. "He does look like he's in less pain."

Before Louise wheeled her husband away for the five-hour drive back to Arlington, I bent on one knee and patted Gene on the back of his hand. "Get well soon!" I said. And although he couldn't speak or yet lift his drooping head, I did see the left side of his mouth rise slightly, and what seemed like a ray of hope flickered in his eye. I smiled back, then reminded his wife of her promise to send me a copy of the postintervention MRI and medical report to add to the body of evidence I had been accumulating. The goal was to document the efficacy of consciousness migrating into another person and manifesting a tangible, benevolent change.

Here is the analogy my brother used to explain the process of transmutation to me. An ice cube will go from a solid to a liquid to a gas as energy from an external "source" is brought to bear in the form of heat that speeds up the motion of the molecules. As more heat is applied, the liquid molecules begin to dance ever faster and eventually transmute to an invisible gas—water vapor. Gary Zukav explained this phenomenon in his book *The Dancing Wu Li Masters*, in which he stated that no matter is really solid, although it appears so, but all matter is really a dancing mass of molecules. In some way, the divine energy being channeled through me was able to transmute the tumor in Gene's brain, releasing lots of heat in the process. I assumed that the energy also succeeded in shrinking the tumor, but I had no evidence of that as yet.

Ten days later I received a phone call from Louise, who sounded much livelier than she had in the past. I asked how Gene was doing.

"He's doing great!" she said with enthusiasm.

"Really?" I said, happy to hear it.

"He's up," she said, "walking by himself, going to the bathroom, talking up a storm. Today he wanted to drive the car! Would you like to speak with him?"

That was a welcome question, as Gene had been unable to say a word when he was in my office. "How do you feel?" I asked him.

"I feel great," he said with a steady voice.

I was thrilled to hear that, but I was also curious about his latest MRI. "Were you able to get me the follow-up medical reports?" I asked.

"No," he said. "When I went back to the NCI, they said that, because I'm no longer being treated—I'm not a surgical candidate, and I'm not responding to chemo and radiation—there was nothing more they felt they could do for me. I'm no longer their patient, so there's no protocol for them to give me another MRI."

I was amazed at what sounded like a classic Catch-22. "Well," I said, "how did your doctor react when you walked back into the office without a wheelchair, weeks later?"

"Oh," Gene said, "my doctor was shocked."

"Then what happened?"

"I asked him if I could get a new MRI, and he explained what I just said—there was no protocol for it. But I said, 'I want to know why I'm walking and I have no pain.' He didn't really have an answer for me."

"Yes, but if it's your desire to get a new MRI," I said, "and you're as eager as I am to see the condition of your tumor, why not just offer to pay for it?"

Apparently Gene hadn't thought of that, but he assured me that he would pursue the possibility right away. He indeed wanted to see MRI results from after his meeting with me.

"Great," I said. "When you get the results, would you please send me a copy?"

It took some time, but Gene and Louise did eventually send me the results of a new MRI, which I will discuss in more detail in Chapter 11.

The day Louise and Gene first came to see me in my office, I experienced a flashback to a time when I felt helpless in much the way Louise sounded and her husband looked, slumped over in his wheelchair. When I was four years old, my dad was seriously injured while fighting a fire. One of the heavy wooden ladders had fallen and struck him in the head. Naturally, I had no way of gauging how dire the situation was, but I took my cues from the adults around me. My mother took me to the hospital to visit Dad and tried to be stoical about it, but I could see how upset she was. He kept going in and out of consciousness, was having balancing problems and trouble standing up. Without MRIs, the doctors had no easy way of diagnosing what was wrong with him, and no reliable course of treatment.

As we drove home from the hospital, my mother was crying. "When can Daddy come home for dinner?" I asked.

"I don't know, Joey," she said. That feeling of helplessness stuck with me for a lifetime. For many months, after he finally did come home, the Fire Department doctors wouldn't give Dad the okay to return to work. The whole experience was one of the driving forces behind my childhood dream of working in healthcare and restoring people's health. I felt that I would do anything to get my dad back safe and sound, and to console my mother as well. That childhood experience instilled in me my first profound sense of empathy, which kicked in without my consciously thinking about it. The same visceral empathic emotion reemerged on the day when I reached out literally to the new kid in my high school by pushing a chair in his direction, and again at the sight of Gene in his wheelchair and the sound of desperation in his wife's voice. Empathy, of course, is natural to all of us, but, as with intuition and other natural gifts, we can learn to develop it. I'll explain more about that process in subsequent chapters. For now it's enough to acknowledge the role it came to play in directing me on my life's path.

## Chapter 6

---

# THE MEASURE OF A MAN'S WORTH

> Not everything that counts can be counted, and not everything that can be counted counts.
> —Sign in Albert Einstein's office at Princeton University

> Let us think of education as the means of developing our greatest abilities, because in each of us there is a private hope and dream which, fulfilled, can be translated into benefit for everyone.
> —John F. Kennedy

In the spring of 1976, my mother served a cake after dinner to celebrate my sixteenth birthday. I felt kind of silly, but at her urging I blew out the candles and made a wish. Yet before the rising smoke from the extinguished candles could dissipate, my dad asked me, "So, young man, what are your plans for the future?"

The very next week, when I arrived at school, I was herded into the assembly room with my entire sophomore class for an orientation to the upcoming Scholastic Aptitude Test, or SAT. This test had been engineered, they assured us, to help us plan our futures by measuring our potential in a scientific manner. I listened carefully as the administrator told us that this was an important point in our lives that would have far-reaching ramifications. We were instructed to get a good night's sleep before the exam, then dismissed with an inspiring quotation based on the great bard's words: "There is a tide in the affairs of young men and women, which, taken at the flood, leads on to fortune; but omitted, your lives will be destined to the doldrums and shallows of existence."

I certainly didn't want my life to be destined to the doldrums and shallows of existence. I came to the conclusion that I would need some coaching in career development, but Mom and Dad were on a budget. So I was glad to learn that, in the event you could not afford a private career coach, one would be provided for you.

Weeks later, the SAT scores having been tabulated and delivered to the administration, I was excited to learn that I had been scheduled for a private audience with the school guidance counselor. The idea was to assist me in developing a plan so that I could succeed in the game of life. My mother was also excited. It seemed as if everything was going to work out for her family after all of the hard work and savings that had enabled her to move her family to a better neighborhood, with the promise of her two boys graduating from high school and getting real careers. In preparation for the big meeting, Mom took me to the factory outlet store that offered quality clothes at a discount and purchased a pair of khaki trousers, a button-down shirt, loafers, and navy blue socks.

On the appointed day, nervous but filled with enthusiasm and, as my mother said, "dressed for success," I arrived at the counselor's office with a legal pad under my arm and two pens to record the notes from this important meeting. I have no idea how many meetings that guidance counselor had had with students over the twenty years he had been entrusted with shaping their lives. On the wall I could see many framed documents testifying to his completion of state-mandated courses and his mastery of the new scientific methods for evaluating students. I had read that tests similar to the SAT were being utilized to measure students' potential in Europe and Japan, after which the student was directed into the occupation at which he or she would be most productive.

When I walked into the counselor's office, his head was buried in a file that I presumed to be mine. I remained standing, waiting for him to look up and shake my hand, ready to make eye contact and a good first impression. But he didn't look up, simply said, "Take a seat. Hmm." He finally raised his head but seemed not to see me, instead looking over my shoulder at the commotion the custodial staff was making pruning weeds outside his window. As I sat self-consciously erect on the plastic orange chair, he asked me if I had given any thought to what I wanted to do with my life. My cotton-polyester-blend trousers caused me to slide back awkwardly on the seat of my pants as I thought about the answer to his question.

"I'm waiting," he said, as if he had to leave soon for dinner with some visiting head of state. I took a breath and began disclosing my private dreams, dreams that I hadn't shared with my mother or dad since I blew out the candles on my cake the week before. I began speaking enthusiastically about a school trip we had taken to the United Nations and how inspired I had been to witness diplomats from all countries seeking solutions to issues confronting the world. I added that this had made me think about possibly working there one day.

His blank stare didn't seem to reflect any endorsement of this career as a good choice for me, so I dug deeper and shared the dream I had harbored since the age of four, when my mother took me to visit my dad in the hospital. At that moment I felt a strong desire to alleviate my mother's suffering and anxiety, and the visit had led me to dream about working in healthcare.

"Your dad's a city fireman?" he asked.

"Yes," I said, but he didn't seem impressed.

"Go on," he said.

"Yes," I said, "my dad's a fireman, and he saves lives in his work, so perhaps I could follow in his footsteps and save people, too, in the field of healthcare." Just imagining it and getting it all out made my excitement grow. It made my dream sound real. I imagined myself as a healthcare professional, walking into the hall of a hospital where a concerned parent was waiting and saying, "I believe we can help your child" or "Your family member is going to be fine!" Yes, it seemed like a career that would work, and I felt a rush of energy up my spine from having clearly expressed for the first time what was in my heart.

Of course, I wasn't sure how to go about realizing either of these dreams, but I was hopeful that my counselor would tell me how to apply to a school to get the training and explain how my parents might be able to afford it. As he began to speak, however, I experienced a disturbing physical reaction. My stomach began to churn, and my throat began to close. He was offering the observation that, although I was apparently bright, I had not on paper shown any great scholastic aptitude. "Quite frankly," he concluded, "those choices are unrealistic."

He looked down at my file and scribbled a notation as he continued droning on. "Your scholastic aptitude scores clearly demonstrate that you don't realistically have what it takes to achieve or excel in either of those professions," he said soberly. "You're bright, in terms of your IQ, but your academic achievement does not measure up. So you are not a viable candidate to even think of applying to a college to prepare for those positions. You are what we call a classic underachiever."

My pulse was racing, and I felt like I had been sucker punched in the abdomen. "Isn't there some way I could—" I don't think he even permitted me to finish my sentence. Before he cut me off, he tapped my file with the back of his hand and dropped it on the pile in front of him, placing his hand on top of it as if it were a Bible and he was solemnly testifying that all the truth he needed to arrive at his conclusion was contained in the pages under his hand. "It's best that you pursue a trade school and get some training to pre-pare for something," he said, pausing briefly as if to come up with the right word, "like a mechanic. And if that doesn't work out" (here he gazed out the window at the men cleaning the grounds) "you could always find gainful employ in custodial work."

As I steadied myself getting out of the chair, he imparted a few final words of advice. "You really need to be realistic," he said matter-of-factly. I felt as if I had been cut off at the knees. I took a step toward the door, the belief in myself I'd had when I entered the room collapsing along with my erect posture. My eyes sank to the floor, fixating on my new loafers as he let his parting shot fly. "You need to set your sights a bit lower." That was the knock-out punch. He had devastated me without placing a hand on me.

With the blood draining from my face, I stepped into his outer office. Three other students were sitting confidently on the edges of their seats, lined up like airplanes on the tarmac, ready to take off on their maiden flights to some unknown destination. As I moved past them lethargically, I began to question my worth in the world. I took this man's expert advice to heart, beginning to accept as truth his worldview that the wisdom of my heart was misleading me. Perhaps I was deluding myself, and perhaps intangible assets that had not been considered in the equation, such as the enthusiasm, passion, and knowing that had served me so well as a child, didn't count. My dreams were just that, mere fantasies, and I should abandon them. By the time I reached the hall, I had already tossed my dreams in the wastepaper basket along with the pad that I had brought to record the good news for my mother. Nor did it occur to me that this highly decorated veteran of the career wars might be wrong. After all, he had sold me on his conclusion based on the science of measuring human aptitude.

I went home that day in a kind of fog and marched right up to my room to change out of my new pants and dress shoes. I didn't want to see my mother that evening, so I skipped dinner. I knew that she'd ask what the guidance counselor had prophesied about my future, and I didn't want to lie to her. My impulse at sixteen was to shield my parents from the collateral damage of my apparent failure. I began to have more appreciation for their sacrifices and to understand that they had worked so hard and struggled to save simply to give their children more opportunity than they had had.

In the weeks that followed, I spent a lot of time in my bedroom with the door closed, experiencing for the first time a private little hell with no understanding or tools to get myself out. When I wasn't at school, I remained indoors, ignoring my friends. My mother was concerned and offered to cook me something special, urged me to see friends, but I had no appetite and felt too numb to do anything.

By a stroke of good fortune, the backyard of our new home abutted on the sprawling Roosevelt Estate. Our modest property was separated from their mansion and grounds by the Browns River, a brackish waterway that extended from the saltwater bay inland, connecting to a string of small lakes that ran north into the heart of Long Island. After a few weeks of hibernating in my room, I started to venture into the marsh behind our home, wearing a pair of NYFD boots that my dad had discarded.

As I made my way through the cattails and reeds to sit by the river, I noticed that at first it was silent. Then as I sat very still, not moving my head and using only my eyes to scan the landscape, the marsh would slowly come alive, first with animal sounds and then with movement in the reeds as the egrets hunted the newly hatched fish seeking sanctuary until they matured and ventured out to the bay. Overhead I learned to recognize the distinctive whistling of the wings of greenwing and cinnamon teal. Soon all sorts of animals made their presence known: otters, raccoons, swans with a train of little cygnets behind them. It was a peaceful place where I could enjoy being alone.

As I learned to be quiet for longer periods of time, my being began to blend into the wild habitat, and the wild seemed to seep into me. I must have spent hundreds of hours in the marsh, just sitting still, until I would drift into a meditative state, even though I didn't really know what that meant back then. I had time on my hands, and, without a dream or purpose, it was easy to just sit in the marsh for hours each day. My grandmother Maude had recently passed away, and as I sat there I remembered the times we used to drive out into the woods to wait for the wildlife to come out. Her words reverberated in my memory: "Just because you can't see them doesn't mean they aren't there. Just be patient." I started to feel that perhaps something at a distance, unseen, was waiting for me, but that I had to be patient for it to reveal itself. And as I remembered my grandmother's lesson, hope started to rekindle in my psyche.

Around that time I watched a documentary about Martin Luther King, Jr.'s "I have a Dream" speech from 1963, which galvanized so many to join the budding civil rights movement. King understood, and made clear for others to see, the detrimental psychological conditioning that permeated society and its institutions. He exposed and identified the origin of the psychological problem he called a "hellhound" that had visited untold harm on and eroded the confidence of millions of people. In later years King singled out the debilitating effects of people being told often enough that they are inferior "to remind them that the lie of their inferiority is accepted as truth in the society dominating them."

At sixteen I was too immature to challenge the validity of a system that was blind to the potential to achieve my dreams. Years later I read the philosopher Bertrand Russell's telling insight on just this subject. "It is because modern education is so seldom inspired by a great hope that it so seldom achieves a great result," he wrote. "The wish to preserve the past rather than the hope of creating the future dominates the minds of those who control the teaching of the young." I had no idea how to undo the mental and spiritual damage that had been inflicted on me by an education system pegged to the past. I longed to reclaim the belief I'd had as a child that all things are possible, a belief that makes life such a profound joy. I missed the confidence that had enabled me to receive guidance and tap into the Source that resides beyond the perceptions of our five senses and the measure of science.

As with my experience in the high school lunchroom, it wasn't until many years later that I understood the true significance of that event. Only after I had been engaged in my pioneering research in consciousness-based healthcare did I finally receive the kind of validation I had been hoping for in my meeting with the guidance counselor. The year was 2007, while I was conducting an outcome study for the Global Health Institute, a foundation I had helped form to advance the integration of conventional healthcare with complementary and alternative modalities, such as consciousness-based healthcare. (I'll give a detailed account of the formation and goals of the institute in Chapter 14.) At the

Global Health Institute we distinguished mind-body medicine from consciousness-based healthcare. The premise behind mind-body medicine, simply put, is that the mind of the patient can have a healing effect on the body of the patient. By contrast, in consciousness-based healthcare the mind of the practitioner can heal the body of the patient.

Mind-body medicine has been growing in acceptance since the mid-twentieth century, based on research showing that modalities such as stress reduction and meditation, visualization, and biofeedback can lower blood pressure and heart rate and have other beneficial effects as well. Although they initially met with resistance from the medical community, most of these practices have now been accepted into the mainstream of conventional medicine and are recommended or practiced by doctors and therapists and in hospitals across the country.

Consciousness-based healthcare represents a quantum leap beyond mind-body medicine in that the consciousness, or nonlocal mind, of the practitioner extends into the body of the person seeking help. This relatively new modality can be applied to reshape a disfigured face, mend broken limbs, shrink a brain tumor (as I described in the previous chapter), or accelerate rehabilitation after surgery or trauma from accidents. As with mind-body medicine early in the last century, consciousness-based healthcare has not yet met with general acceptance.

The medical advisory board of the foundation decided we would conduct a pilot study to evaluate the efficacy of consciousness-based healthcare applied to the face. We worked with nineteen participants to evaluate the evidence of treatment effect by taking photographs of their faces before and after treatments for issues ranging from severe disfigurement to the effects of bad surgery and aging. Some subjects were suffering from genetic disorders, such as temporal band syndrome, while others had facial scars caused by surgery, car accidents, or dog bites. Still other participants were simply seeking cosmetic improvements that did not entail the risks associated with conventional surgery. The preliminary evaluation was carried out by three in-house researchers, who found evidence of positive effects in all nineteen post-intervention outcome photographs. Among the researchers was Dr. Frank Salvatore, a board-certified urologist involved in clinical practice for over twelve years. Dr. Salvatore had by his own admission "become increasingly frustrated by the limitations of the management options for prostate cancer." That experience, he said, had "propelled my interest into alternative and comple-mentary therapies, and for the last five years I have been seeking out a vehicle for me to make a contribution over and above what I am currently able to do in my traditional urologic practice."

The photographs in the study were further evaluated by an outside, unpaid diplomate of the American Board of Plastic Sur-gery, who was "blinded," not informed of the modality used to achieve the results. He determined that more than 90 percent of the participants had undergone noticeable change and had achieved their desired result. These extraordinarily significant evaluations inspired us to undertake further studies.

I subsequently discussed the results of our study at a dinner party at which a number of noted philanthropists were meeting with some venture capitalists looking to invest in worthy projects. Among the philanthropists was Ellen Scarborough, who took an immediate interest in what I had said, and asked if she could help in any way. I thanked her for her openness and added that I needed people who above all practice true philanthropy, which is divorced from ego. I said that when Michelangelo sculpted, for example, he gave credit to the Source. He said that the power that flows from the Divine could conquer nature. Ellen replied that her dear friend Luciano Pavarotti also gave credit to Spirit for his brilliant operatic performances. "Pavarotti always said that he was just a conduit for the Divine," she said.

I was delighted that she understood precisely what I was getting at.

"So," Ellen repeated, "how can I be of service?"

"We need people to participate in our studies under the auspices of medical doctors," I said, and I explained how an outcome study works. Ellen liked the idea and agreed to come to our office. She specifically wanted to know how she could help advance the integration of consciousness-based therapies. As she spoke so enthusiastically, it occurred to me that her affect and spirit seemed much younger than her physical age, based on appearances. "You have the spirit of a twenty-five-year-old," I said, "but your exterior appearance doesn't reflect that spirit."

Ellen agreed that she more or less looked her age. "Why don't I bring in a photo or two from twenty years ago, when I was thirty years old?" she said, suggesting that we could use that for contrast. We set up a meeting for the following week.

Ellen Ward Scarborough turned out to have a fascinating backstory. Born in suburban Chicago as a Daughter of the American Revolution (whose members can "prove lineal descent from a patriot of the American Revolution"), she earned a college degree in history and won an independent fellowship to study architectural historic preservation in London. Ellen subsequently studied art history, art, and architecture at institutions including the Parsons school of design in Paris, worked as an interior designer, and is now a highly regarded antiques dealer. A fixture on the Connecticut and Manhattan social scenes, Ellen has long been involved with the Animal Rescue Fund of the Hamptons and other humane organizations.

Ellen showed up as scheduled with her husband. She brought the photos and told me that, when she was thirty, her nose was less bulbous and didn't droop, as it now plainly did. I explained the reasons for that development as succinctly as I could. In his book *Radical Healing: Integrating the World's Great Therapeutic Traditions to Create a New Transformative Medicine*, Dr. Rudolph Ballentine described how a plaque called amma becomes lodged in the subcutaneous layers of the skin. When we're younger that material is easily flushed away, but as we age the body is not as efficient at removing the buildup of debris. In my experience, once it's removed, the face becomes more defined and taut, especially under the ridge of the brow, underneath the eyes and the jaw, and around the chin.

Ellen's husband asked well-formed, probing questions about the work we would be doing and whether there would be medical supervision. Frank Salvatore, then the director of clinical studies at the Global Health Institute, explained that he was a board-certified surgeon and would be observing throughout. Then Ellen's husband asked if the work could have unintended after-effects, and I explained that the process had never demonstrated negative effects. But, he wanted to know, how was it possible that he had never heard about a way to make noninvasive changes to the features of the face?

Dr. Salvatore said that this was indeed a very new development, but that it was in line with the evolution of medical science. In the past, for instance, surgeons had to perform invasive surgery to remove kidney stones. Nowadays, through a process called lithotripsy, they can send high-energy shock waves into the body to dissolve those stones without the risks associated with invasive surgery. After this noninvasive procedure, the tiny pieces of stones can pass painlessly out of the body in the urine. In effect, we would be taking that concept to the next level. Instead of shock waves, we would be focusing human intention to diminish and taper the bulbous nose, shrinking and lifting the tip.

"I'm not familiar with that concept," Ellen's husband said. I suggested that he read Dr. Larry Dossey's *Reinventing Medicine: Beyond Mind-Body to a New Era of Healing* and Dr. Ballentine's *Radical Healing*, and with that he seemed comfortable. Ellen then showed us her photos from a couple of decades before. "You can see that, when I was younger, my chin was more defined and I had a nice diminutive nose," she pointed out.

"Fine," I said. "I need you to hold in your heart and mind what your heart desires, whatever that may be."

"Oh," she said with a broad smile, "I know how I'd like to look!"

"Then hold that thought," I said.

In order to have a before-and-after record, a series of high-resolution images were taken using a Sony camera outfitted with a Carl Zeiss lens, the kind favored by plastic surgeons because it does not alter skin tone. The consent forms were signed, and it was time to begin.

Once Ellen was lying on the table, I began to focus my intention on the issues that she had pointed out in her face, primarily the nose. I sat on a stool, and Dr. Salvatore stood behind me so that he could watch over my shoulder. As Ellen's face began to morph into the look she wanted, Dr. Salvatore started to emit whistling sounds. "Whew! I've seen the medical application," he said, referring to the process, "but this is the first time I'm witnessing the cosmetic work."

Twenty minutes later, I handed Ellen a mirror and asked her and Dr. Salvatore to testify on video what changes they could observe.

"Oh, my goodness, this is unbelievable," Ellen said.

"Look at that," Dr. Salvatore said. "Look at the chin."

"The chin is amazing!" Ellen said.

"Do you remember?" Dr. Salvatore said. "Oh, my God."

"Ellen, what do you see in the shape of the chin?" I asked.

"It's much more defined," she said, "and the skin looks much smoother and tauter."

"And the tip of the nose?"

"The tip of the nose is like marble, polished marble."

Ellen said that her nose now looked like it had when she was thirty-five. She later told me that when she saw her sister for the first time after having worked with me, her sister said, "You look like when you got married fifteen years ago."

# Chapter 7

## A VOICE IN THE MIST

We are evolving from five-sensory humans into multisensory humans. . . . The perceptions of the multisensory human extend beyond physical reality.

—Gary Zukav

Prayer is not an old woman's idle amusement. Properly understood and applied, it is the most potent instrument of action.

—Mohandas Gandhi

I was asleep, but my sense of hearing registered the alarm, pulling me out of my slumber. I came awake from my dream state, but my eyes remained closed, recognizing that the sound waking me was my bedside alarm clock. I reached over and slapped the switch on top, silencing the alarm. I had slept a bit longer than I should have, because I had stayed up late the evening before to celebrate with my classmates our recent graduation from Bayport High School. I was still a bit tired and under the weather, but, realizing that I was running behind schedule for my summer job, I popped my eyes open and tossed the sheet in the air with my arm. My legs bounced off the bed, I landed on the floor with both feet, and before the sheet drifted back to the mattress, I was heading down the stairs in my cutoffs and T-shirt.

While many of the other kids in my new neighborhood had summer internships with law firms and Wall Street trading companies, my dad didn't have those professional connections. So, with his ultimatum to get a summer job, I had figured I would use whatever talents God had given me. With my decent swimming ability learned from Dad and my growth spurt over the previous winter, at age seventeen I was already a big six feet, one inch and 190 pounds but still a kid at heart. I had taken the Suffolk County ocean lifeguard exam and landed a job at the public beach known as Smith Point on Fire Island National Seashore. Now, with the hands moving on the face of my scuba diving watch, a graduation gift from my grandfather, I threw some lunch in my backpack, jumped in my ten-year-old Ford, still running but on its last legs, and set out for the early morning drive east on Sunrise Highway toward Mastic Beach. I turned south onto William Floyd Parkway, stopped for a supersize coffee to help me wake up, and drove the last couple of miles to the bridge that separates the mainland of Long Island from the thirty-two-mile-long barrier beach called Fire Island.

By the time I got to the lifeguard station, all of the other guards had arrived and were swapping their street clothes for the kelly green bathing suits with bold white stripes that served as our uniforms. After suiting up each morning, we made our way down to the beach, but today we were confronted by a real novelty. The thickening fog coalesced on us, clinging to the mustaches of the older veterans and painting opaque masks on the peach fuzz on the faces of the younger guys, like me. We carried with us the tools of the lifeguard trade—lifesaving flotation devices called torpedoes, buckets of coiled rope, Army surplus stretchers, and resuscitation equipment that we were trained to use in the unthinkable event of a drowning.

The next step of the lifeguard routine was to perform our obligatory morning workout. Each day the captain would designate a different guard to select the drill. Given my fatigue from the graduation party, I hoped the designated leader for that morning would select a less arduous workout. Just then something happened that had never happened before: the captain looked at his clipboard and announced, "Farrell, Joe Farrell, you're workout leader this morning." Then the captain cut out two guards to remain with the lifesaving gear at the main tower until the other thirty-three returned to erect the remaining six or seven towers. I could feel all eyes and ears turned my way. They were like a football team huddled around the quarterback, waiting for him to call the play. The options typically were swim workouts; leg-strength workouts consisting of repeatedly carrying a man up a sand dune, called "dunies"; lifesaving drills; or, the most arduous, long-distance runs in the soft sand to build endurance, usually reserved for days when big crowds weren't expected and we had more time to train. I reviewed the options in my mind and was about to call out a swim, as I wasn't one of the best at leg-strength drills and distance runs but I was a good swimmer. That would also provide a refreshing wakeup from last night.

I was just about to shout, "Swim to the sandbar and back," when something stopped me, an inner calling that I could not sense with my ears but that felt as compelling as the alarm clock that had awakened me just an hour before—so urgent, so clear was its message, that I was compelled to act on it. And before my rational mind could stop me, I blurted out, "Run workout east. Push-ups, sprint back!" A muffled chorus of boos emanated from the guards, who like me had celebrated the night before and had hoped for a fast swim before work.

The captain looked at me. "Farrell," he barked, "back in thirty minutes!" And with that the crew took off like a lineup of race-horses sprinting from the gate, looking for the inner track near the water's edge. They all wanted to find that sweet, narrow stretch of hardened sand that provided the best running condi-tions. Some of the faster runners began pulling ever so slightly in front of me, their bare feet sending plumes of ocean water spray-ing up with each strike. As I noticed some of the guys beginning to disappear into the mist ahead, I dug a little deeper and tried to keep up. The front-runners stopped at the turnaround mark, and as the rest of us arrived, some guys took a quick seat in the sand while others shook their legs out. By my watch we had three min-utes before we had to set off on the sprint back to be ready for the anticipated crowds.

Suddenly the coffee that I had consumed on the drive to work made it necessary to answer the call of nature, so I wandered down to the water's edge and went about my business. As I looked to my right and left, I saw the second strange thing that day. Fifty feet from me was a large, mysterious shape. I moved closer and saw that the amorphous form was an off-road camper truck stuck in the surf line. Its cab precariously half in the water with its rear end on the beach, it balanced like some kid's teeter toy. Except that, if it slipped, it would fall right into the ocean.

As I approached to take a better look, I read two bumper stick-ers proclaiming JUST RETIRED and GOD ANSWERS PRAYERS. I walked down the left-hand side of the vehicle, and inside the cab I saw an old woman, her eyes closed, hands clasped together in prayer and lips murmuring as I recalled my grandmother Maude used to do.

In front of the truck, down on all fours, was an old white-haired man with a small folding shovel, attempting to dig out the left wheel. Given the gravity of the situation, I couldn't fathom why the woman sat praying in the truck rather than physically helping. *For God's sake,* I thought. *What does she think she could accomplish by praying?*

I shook my head. As I was taking in their predicament, the man turned his head, and his eyes met mine. "Can I help?" I asked, looking into his red, sweaty face. I could see the fear in his bloodshot eyes and sensed the fatigue in his body. From the look of him, he must have been a powerful man many years ago. "Well, you're a big kid," he replied, although next to the four-by-four pickup truck with camper that weighed close to three tons I must have seemed like a dwarf. "But unless you've got a tow truck, I'm afraid I'm going to lose my retirement home into the rising sea in about five minutes."

I saw the man's CB radio on the dash. "Have you called the park rangers?" I said.

"Yes," he said with a tone of despair. His voice and the look on his face told me that he knew no tow truck would make it in time from the nearest ranger station. But at that moment I had a flash of inspiration. After all, just a few feet away were thirty-two lifeguards in peak physical condition. Maybe together we could lift the truck! I rushed back through the fog to the crew. Having just finished their push-ups, they were standing and brushing the sand off their hands, some stretching in preparation for the two-mile sprint back. "Hey, guys!" I shouted. "Come on, we're going to do a good deed."

As I explained the situation, I could see in their eyes that most of them were not inclined to accept. Some shook their heads and looked back toward the beach. "Come on," I pleaded. "It will just take a minute. They're right over here." I pointed into the fog;

some heads turned, but they could not see the truck teetering on the shelf as the water rose about it. The will of the group was also teetering—in favor of running back to Smith Point. Logically speaking, we were out of our jurisdiction. We had left the county beach and were on the national seashore, where the federal park rangers were responsible for such situations. The guards also knew that, if they didn't get back in time to open the beach, they would catch flak from the chief and maybe even risk termination. My eyes met those of one of the senior guards, named Larry, and bore right into him. I didn't say anything but silently hoped, based on the hint of a sympathetic look in his eye, that he might second my motion.

Just then Larry spoke up. "Come on, guys," he said with spirit. "Come on, let's do this!"

Larry clapped his hands, and with our two wills aligned, we tipped the collective will of the thirty-one guards who were undecided. The decision made, we acted as one. We sprinted into the mist and within seconds had encircled the sinking vehicle, fifteen on the left, fifteen on the right, and three on the front bumper. My hands plunged under the water, fingers searching for a secure handhold. We now stood knee-deep in seawater. Larry's brother, the biggest of all the guards, was at my right shoulder, and as he dug his feet in and flattened his body against the right door, pressing his shoulder to the metal, he looked like some amazing sumo wrestler. We all put our backs into it and shared the enthusiasm for the task. It may have seemed like an impossible challenge, but I did the math: thirty-three guards, each with the capacity to carry a two-hundred-pound adult out of the slick grip of the sea, amounted to over six thousand pounds of lifting power, enough for the job. More important, I *believed* we could do it, and I smiled inside.

One of the older guys, who had worked the beach for years,

took command. "On three we lift," he said. As he called out "one," I felt the metal bite into my hands; at "two" I could see both arms of the big guy to my right tense; and on *"three!"* a collective groan erupted as all of our legs strained to straighten and our feet sank deeper into the water. The truck that had been buried up to its axle began to lift out of the lapping sea. It went up awkwardly as guys shifted their grips. The old woman still perched inside looked out at us. Her eyes wide with wonder and her mouth open, she held on for dear life as the front of the truck rose four feet into the air, carrying her with it. We hadn't even asked her to get out, but hey, what was another 130 pounds?

Then, as if the truck were some huge centipede that had sprouted countless legs, we ran it up the incline to drop it on the dry beach as draining seawater puddled around it. There was no time for the luxury of self-congratulation. The entire crew on both sides of the truck reacted with one mind. As if they were a herd of wild mustangs spooked by some unseen predator, they bolted from around the truck and tore off, feet digging into the sand. I looked back for a second at the truck sitting safely on the beach. One of the lifeguards standing to my right spun and dug hard into the sand with his foot, throwing grains of sand into the air and pelting the back of my neck and legs. I raised my forearm to shield my eyes as the crew disappeared into the veil of fog from which they had emerged minutes before. When I put my arm down again, for the second time that morning the old man looked into my eyes. But now the fear was gone, replaced by a gratitude that clearly left him speechless, the tiny folding shovel dangling from his hand.

I was the last boy standing there, and my mind began to register that I could lose my job for this stunt if I did not make it back with the rest of the guys. As I smiled at him, I started to walk backward, then to backpedal faster, still holding his gaze. He was clearly in shock, and I knew that in a moment he would come around, but I also knew that I couldn't remain for even another ten seconds to permit him and his wife, now climbing out of the truck with a big smile on her face, the opportunity to express their gratitude. So I waved, turned my back to them, and took off running as fast as I could, to save my own bacon now.

As that old couple traveled to various national parks, they must have had a great time telling the bizarre story of thirty-three men who appeared out of the mist one morning to lift their truck from the clutches of the sea, only to disappear moments later back into the mist. For me, though, the story was a little less satisfying. Einstein may have said, "The most beautiful and profound emotion we can experience is the sensation of the mystical," but the sensation that guided me to act that day seemed more like a source of confusion. As I ran the two miles back, I thought that perhaps I had done something foolish and that I was going to lose my job. I would soon be an adult, and, as my guidance counselor had so bluntly advised me, I would have to begin to listen to reason. So I chose for the second time in my life to run, to turn my back on my spiritual potential and ignore a mystical impulse that had compelled me to lead thirty-two lifeguards down the beach that day. And I would keep running until my soul finally rebelled one day and I could run no more. "Most people," wrote the psychologist William James, "make use of a very small portion of their possible consciousness, and of their Soul's resources in general."

# Chapter 8

## FOOL'S GOLD

With unfailing kindness, your life
always presents what you need to learn.
—Charlotte Joko Beck


For what shall it profit a man, if he shall
gain the whole world, and lose his own
soul?
—*Mark 8:36*


All that glistens is not gold.
—William Shakespeare,
*The Merchant of Venice*


My dream of pursuing a career in the healing profession having
been abandoned on the advice of my high school guidance counselor, I needed to come up with an alternate plan to prepare for
my adulthood. I drifted through my senior year of high school

like a ship without a rudder. And like a ship in a storm, I was looking for favorable conditions and a friendly port to steer toward.
After high school, my older brother, Jake, had enrolled in the New
York Maritime College to study engineering, eventually landing
an engineering officer's job in the Merchant Marine and receiving
a commission in the U.S. Navy.

I took a more mundane course through the maritime college,
learning the business and legalities of international shipping. And
during the summer semester, we went to sea on a training ship,
learning the skills that we'd need to pilot ships of unlimited ton-
nage in any ocean. The four years I attended maritime college,
the oil companies were raking in record profits; one of the most
coveted positions graduates could aspire to was piloting oil super-
tankers like the *Exxon Valdez*. The oil companies needed maritime
officers to navigate these vessels, which could be as long as three
football fields, skillfully enough to limit tearing their fragile sin-
gle-skin hulls. I was on track to become an officer, with the potential of using my skills to command a merchant ship or entering
the armed forces to pilot ships of war. I could even transfer into
aviation and learn to pilot planes. But most of us were more interested in the commercial careers that a course of training in the
maritime college could prepare us for. The Merchant Marine is
primarily responsible for transporting cargo and passengers during peacetime, although in time of war it's considered an auxil-
iary to the Navy, and its ships can be commandeered to deliver
troops and supplies for the military. Still, it's generally not a uni-
formed service, and none of us were expecting war to be declared
anytime soon.

Then an unanticipated thing happened. Ronald Reagan was
president, and we were suddenly facing the distinct possibility of
going to war in the Middle East. I was nearing the four years I had
signed up for when I received a copy of a letter sent on my behalf

to the U.S. Coast Guard from the maritime college at Fort Schuyler, stating that I had completed my course of study and would be graduating that summer. Shortly thereafter, it was announced that all of the cadet midshipmen at the maritime college would assemble the next afternoon at 1500 hours (3:00 P.M.) in the quad to take an oath—an oath that conveyed to the government the right to conscript us into the Navy "if such a commission is tendered," presumably in time of declared war. This eventuality hadn't been brought to my attention during the enrollment process, although it was probably tucked away in the back of the manual. As you can imagine, it came as a surprise and a bit of a shock to me.

And to many other students, too, who had enrolled in the school with every intention of pursuing careers at sea or in the air but not in the military. Just about everyone else in my class took the oath, however, gambling that the United States wouldn't enter into armed conflict. As I learned, graduates of the regimental system were greatly prized by both the armed forces and the maritime industry, as they were by captains of industry—and they all utilized the same regimental chain of command. If the midshipmen were well trained, orders from the bridge of a ship or the boardroom of a corporation would be executed without question and in perfect, conscienceless obedience.

I remember the moment vividly. I had to decide whether to take the mandatory oath to accept a commission in the armed forces if one were tendered. At that, my soul rebelled; my inner essence felt aligned more with being a healer than with being a warrior. I walked into the administrative office and saluted the officer. "Sir," I said, "could you please help me to understand what this oath is that we're being asked to take tomorrow, and the phrase 'must agree in writing to apply for a commission.'"

"It's nothing to be nervous about," I was told. "Typically the

Navy doesn't exercise its option; it only does so if some need exists, and then only chooses officers with leadership potential." The officer looked up from the paperwork on his desk, took in the six-foot-one frame that I had inherited from my dad, and the three gold bars on my lapel, which had been bestowed on me in my fourth year in recognition of leadership quality, and he smiled like a big Cheshire cat. From that tell, he tipped his cards, and I got the drill perfectly.

"Anything else?"

"No, sir, that will be all."

I felt betrayed, like a pawn in some scheme I didn't fully understand. Now that I had to decide on my own what to do, I paid a visit to the registrar. An older woman in a crisp business suit, the registrar pulled out my file, placed it on the counter, and handed me my university diploma. I admired the blue and gold motif and seal. I told her that a future in the maritime service was unfortunately not in the stars for me, though, and that I wanted to seek a different path. Her eyebrow raised, she smiled and gave me a kind look and a pout. "But you've come so far," she said. Then she gently retrieved the college degree with my name on it from my grasp, slid it back into its jacket, and tapped the file with her index finger.

"Okay, young man," she said. "We'll hold on to this for you in case you change your mind."

I thanked her and said I didn't think I'd be back again. I removed the three gold bars from my collar, placed them on the counter, and bid her adieu. However, I kept my medical corpsman's pin, which held a deeper significance for me as part of my ongoing dream of working in healthcare. As a medical corpsman in the maritime college, I had received some training in emergency medicine, watching the physicians work and learning the most basic tasks, like taking blood pressure and treating heat exhaustion. So I was proud of that pin and what it represented in my journey.

Ten days later, the commissions were handed out and the sea of faces and bodies stood at attention in rows as we had been indoctrinated to do on the first day. Cheering young male and female midshipman cadets listened to words of inspiration from the valedictorian and then flung their caps into the air. I was not to be seen among their ranks.

.

During the last year that I had been away at maritime college, I returned from sea to learn that my parents had divorced and sold their beloved home on Long Island, and that my pride and joy, my yellow Lab, had jumped the fence and run away. My life felt like chaos. My dad still had a beach cottage out on the island, though, and he also kept a modest apartment on the Upper East Side, which he let me use as I embarked on a new career. Having jumped ship from the Merchant Marine, I signed on to an occupation that could prove militaristic in its own way: working in the competitive New York City real estate market. When I started living on the East Side, I was amazed by the outward glamour and glitz, the private helicopters, luxury cars, and posh apartments encircling Central Park West and South, up and down Fifth Avenue, Park, and Madison. It seemed that it was no longer about asking what you could do for your country but asking what you could grab for yourself. It was the heyday of men who were altering the look of the skyline, memorializing their names on the façades of residential buildings, hospitals, casinos, and even the tails of their jets.

In this time of fiscal bacchanal, I devoured books like *The Art of the Deal* and set my course for the upper echelons of the real estate game. At the maritime college I had learned a lot more than steering by the stars and lifeboat drills. I had also studied the nuts and bolts of trade and the law of international commerce, giving me a grasp of business fundamentals. I knew, for instance, that offer and acceptance equals a legal contract, which consists of a meeting of the minds for any legal transfer of goods or services.

But what you are taught in school is not how the game of business is fought in the trenches, as I would soon learn. College business studies present a world akin to gentleman's boxing with gloves, whereas corporate business is more like bare-fisted street fighting with no rules. In short order I was taught that the motivational tactics I should employ to be a success in the industry consisted primarily of fear, need, and greed.

You instilled fear in your customers by letting them know that, if they didn't act fast, they would lose out. If they were hesitating over a deal, you were to inform them you expected a bid later in the day, as one of my first bosses told me. "Make up a person!" he said. "Say that Mr. Longchamp is returning with an anticipated offer to purchase that same condo."

The second rule was to make your customers need you, not necessarily because of the service you provide but for the status or cachet you convey. "Tell them they need this luxury apartment," my boss would say. "Make them believe that, if you don't have a place in New York City, you're a nobody."

And always play on their greed. If you learned that a couple had just gotten a divorce, or was heading for one, that represented a great opportunity to take advantage of misfortune. For some reason, I didn't think about it. I just jumped in with both feet. I was singled out as having the potential to make vast amounts of money and was told to forget what I'd learned about business in college. "This isn't school," my boss loved to say. "This is the real world."

I was twenty-four, just a year out of college, and had bought my first suit and briefcase. I decided to take some night courses in real estate investment and finance at Pace University, and by day I made real estate deals. I worked at the same firm off and on for a couple of years, until something happened that soured me on the whole business. I had been referred to a VIP client, a medical doctor who had devoted himself to cancer research, which had led to a discovery with the potential to save many lives. As a result, he had won a prestigious award and was leaving for Scandinavia to receive his prize. But on his return he was going to need an office to archive the results of his work and prepare papers for publication—and he would need it right away. I spent the morning looking at available units with him and was delighted when he chose one that would perfectly suit his needs. He made an offer, which I submitted and the landlord accepted. I took the doctor's check for a deposit in good faith. We had a meeting of the minds, agreed on price consideration, made an offer, and had it accepted. Hence, we had a contract. Or so I thought.

To celebrate, the doctor insisted on taking me to lunch, where he told me how pleased he was that I'd been able to help him. But in truth nobody was more pleased than I was. In a job that didn't offer many nonmaterial rewards, the thought of having been able to help someone involved in valuable work like cancer research, who also happened to be a kind, generous human being, made me feel better than I had in a long time. Just after he left for the airport, I received a call from my boss telling me that he had just gotten an offer from another client for $250 a month more for the same unit. He instructed me to call my client and tell him that his lease had been canceled.

I explained that the landlord had already accepted his offer and that I had the doctor's good faith deposit. "Just lie," my boss said matter-of-factly. "Tell him it's your mistake, but you weren't aware

that a previous offer for more money had already been accepted."
I said I just couldn't do that. My boss explained that if I didn't do
as I was told, I'd be fired. Instead of waiting for that to happen, a
few days later I handed in my resignation.

I went back to Pace to take more courses and applied for a job
at one of New York City's oldest real estate firms. This company
had an air of integrity, with an office on Madison Avenue, and I
clicked with them. I made a lot of money in the time I worked
there, but somehow it all felt like some kind of glossy Hollywood
movie that left me as empty as ever. As I looked at my face in the
mirror each day, I saw it hardening, the light in my eyes dimming.
Yet I survived, and what was not killing me was making me better
at this game—at a cost. I began to prosper materially, but, unbeknownst to me, I was losing my soul, my inner light, in the bar-
gain.

What made this realization even more painful was my growing awareness that I was surrounded by people who were even
less concerned about other people than I feared I was becoming.
My eyes were opened wide to the level of desperation and amo-
rality driving my colleagues by a deal I made for a wealthy buyer
from Italy who was seeking an investment property. If I could
find him something suitable, it would mean a sizable commission,
so I worked with him over the Christmas holidays for torturous
hours, showing properties and making offers and counteroffers.
We finally reached a meeting of minds and closed a deal on a
property for $1.3 million. I submitted the paperwork to the cor-
porate office, including the senior staffer who gave me the listing
for the referral fee of 1 percent due her. I also entered my name as
the broker of record, for which I would be due 4 percent.

I left the city to spend the last day of the holidays with my folks
and returned to discover that the senior staffer had switched our
names on the paperwork. She listed herself as the broker who

had negotiated the deal and left me with just the finder's fee. This amounted to fraud, and I marched into the president's office to inform him of the unethical switcheroo. He said he would look into it and proceeded to sweep the affair under the rug. When I later confronted him about his inaction, he told me that, because the senior staffer made more money for the firm than I did, he had to side with her—as if it were just a difference of opinion. Nothing personal, just business, he said.

I felt like someone whose spouse had cheated on him. Trust was destroyed, and without trust the relationship was forever tainted. When I confronted the woman who had taken my commission, she said it was a matter of necessity. She was buying a luxury home in Greenwich and needed the money that I had earned to put toward the down payment. I didn't know how to seek recourse and management didn't care. As Gandhi said, "Morality is contraband in war." So we were at war, and ethics was of no importance to the corporate bottom line.

I was climbing the corporate ladder but leaving chunks of my soul behind. As I reviewed my growing assets and portfolio of properties, and the mounting connections I was making, I realized I could soon be near the top. I began to be invited to parties at places like the Rainbow Room. This paragon of posh celebration, located on the sixty-fifth floor of the GE Building in Rockefeller Center, is known, among other things, for a dance floor that revolves slowly while a live band plays elegant music. At the peak of one party there, Tony Bennett sang "New York, New York" as a special present for the birthday of a major real estate titan. The man applauded Tony, who gave him a slight bow of recognition before walking off, as classy as could be. I stood there watching the famous circular dance floor rotate as couples danced with glazed eyes, reveling in their pursuit and celebration of material gain. But instead of being filled with awe, I felt a sudden vertigo.

It was like watching wooden horses on a carousel—and I realized that I was becoming one of them.

Meanwhile, each morning as I walked to work, I would pass the Manhattan Eye, Ear, and Throat Hospital, where the cranio-facial experts were helping to repair and elevate lives. I grew more despondent and started to go to work less and to the gym more often. Exercise was the only thing that made me feel alive. One day, a woman who was stretching on the mat next to me asked me what sport I played. She was doing a split and stretching with such ease, yet she surprised me by asking if I was a dancer. "No," I said. "Two left feet."

When she asked if I liked dance, I had to admit I'd never been to the ballet. "I do think that dancers are some of the best ath-letes in the world, though," I added. "And I appreciate the mas-tery." We laughed, and she said that she was a ballet dancer. In her floppy cotton sweats and T-shirt, I figured she was a student at one of the local dance schools. She asked if I'd like to come to the ballet someday, because she occasionally got complimentary tickets. I gave her my business card, and when I went to my office a few days later, there was a ticket to the New York City Ballet waiting for me.

It turned out to be a great seat in the third row, and I was sit-ting next to some elegant women who looked like they lived at the theater. We struck up a conversation, and I asked if they knew a dancer named Darci Kistler. I was surprised to learn they were quite familiar with Darci, so I asked if they'd point her out to me when she came on. I imagined she'd be back in the corps somewhere. But then an enormous oyster was rolled onstage, it opened up, and out stepped a beautiful woman with very long hair. It was Darci. The humble young woman from the gym was George Balanchine's prima ballerina. I was enchanted seeing my new acquaintance light up the stage. She moved to a corner, gathered herself down low, took several powerful strides, and then propelled her long body into the air, her legs going into a perfect split, her toes piercing the air like the tip of an arrow. As she continued to rise, her arms came up to the horizontal, her fingertips so loose that a butterfly could have nested between her fingers and not damaged its wings.

Darci turned to the audience smiling, a sparkle coming from her eyes, as if she were infused with something spiritual. And for that moment, which seemed to last a long time, the crowd was transported into the air with her. She had convinced the audience that it was possible for a woman to fly. Perhaps this woman didn't have the business connections that others had, but she definitely had a connection to the Divine.

Two weeks later Darci asked me if I would be her date for the New York City Ballet Dance with the Dancers event, at which benefactors could dine in Lincoln Center's opera house with the beautiful crystal chandeliers. At dinner, Peter Martins, the balletmaster of the troupe, came over to check on one of his top dancers and her mystery date. When Darci introduced me, Martins asked what I did for a living. "Real estate brokerage and appraisal," I said, pretty much as I had to a previous date's wealthy father.

"Oh well," he said, turning to Darci, "we will forgive him that."

I hadn't yet cultivated an appreciation for the art of sarcasm, but even in my naïveté I got the picture. As a broker, a merchant, I was seen as an interloper at the table of his muses in this temple built from reverence for the arts. He somehow made me feel all right about it later, but I knew what he meant, and I was inclined to agree.

I saw Darci dance once more after that, and after the performance we ran across the street to the Ginger Man for a late supper. I asked Darci about her inspiration, and she said she was a spiritual person, a devout believer in God. The great thing about

Darci was that her success had nothing to do with wanting to make piles of money or be world famous. "When I dance," she said, "if I'm doing it right, everyone's burdens are lifted in a moment of grace." She said that without a hint of conceit or self-importance but with a simple knowing that she was part of the divine plan, and that her success was as much the result of hard work and desire as of somehow by the grace of God tapping into the energy of the universe. "When inspiration strikes," she said, "regardless of the time, you need to embrace it."

Afterward I realized that she was saying in her own words what the great composer Johann Sebastian Bach intended when he inscribed "SDG" at the end of many of his musical manuscripts. Those initials stand for *Soli Deo Gloria*, Latin for "Glory to God alone." You can feel the peace and equanimity in the least of Bach's preludes, but in his larger works it can be all but overwhelming. The acclaimed actress and legendary teacher Uta Hagen said in her book *Respect for Acting* that the stage performer can be a social activist by working to bring others to a higher place.

Before we left the restaurant, Darci said five words that shifted my life path. "You can't work for money." Whatever you do in life, she explained, has to come from more than financial motivation.

Some time later I had begun seeing a woman who represented the other end of the spectrum from Darci. She came from an enormously wealthy family and had made it clear that, if we married, I would be set for life. When I brought the woman to visit my dad at his beach cottage, they really hit it off. Besides being rich, she was quite charming and beautiful, and my dad was impressed that my prospects seemed to be shaping up. By that time, however, I had already begun to have second thoughts about this woman, whose main concern in life seemed to be maintaining the privileged lifestyle in which she had been raised. All of her friends shared her preoccupation and looked down on anyone who wasn't part of their social set. So when my dad took me aside to say that he thought we made a nice couple, and asked if I intended to marry her, I said it was unlikely.

"You must be crazy," he said with real frustration. "I don't understand you. Why in heaven would you pass up such a life?"

His comments reminded me of a story I had read in Yogananda's wonderful book *Autobiography of a Yogi*. A highly respected spiritual teacher was known to have forsaken enormous family wealth in his early childhood, choosing instead to become a yogic master. One of his students says to him, "Master, you are wonderful! You have renounced riches and comforts to seek God and teach us wisdom!" But the teacher isn't having any of it.

"You are reversing the case," he replies in a mild rebuke. "I have left a few paltry rupees, a few petty pleasures, for a cosmic empire of endless bliss. How then have I denied myself anything? I know the joy of sharing the treasure. Is that a sacrifice? The shortsighted worldly folk are verily the real renunciates! They relinquish an unparalleled divine possession for a poor handful of earthly toys! The divine order arranges our future more wisely than any insurance company."

Unfortunately for me, I hadn't yet fully embraced that master's faith in the divine order. While I continued to work for money, I also felt disappointed that I hadn't pursued my childhood dream of helping people through healthcare. My conflicted feelings were subconsciously draining my energy. I lost my drive to work and began to feel very low energy. So when my friend Wendy invited me to join her in Brooklyn, I immediately perked up. She had heard about a woman from South America who was a mystic and was full of great love and empathy. I got the feeling Wendy didn't feel safe going to see her alone, so I agreed to accompany her, not really knowing what to expect. Wendy explained that the woman was the disciple of a South American shaman and that she could heal many illnesses but that day she was going to perform spiritual blessings.

When we arrived, we were led into a room with about a dozen people, mostly women, sitting on couches and the floor while a small fountain bubbled away in the background. I watched this woman, whom Wendy called simply Maria, sit with each person in the room. And with a tremendous amount of love emanating toward these perfect strangers, she seemed to help them. I watched the woman to whom Maria just whispered a few words burst out crying; they seemed to elicit a powerful cathartic release. Maria's interpreter then pointed at me, and I came over to receive whatever she was offering.

Maria looked at me intently and with an expression of concern. Her interpreter asked if anything was bothering me, and I said, "Yes. My medical doctor says I'm depressed." The woman translated, and Maria gave me a great big smile, shaking her head slowly back and forth. "No," she said through her interpreter, "nothing is wrong with you. You're just not doing what you're supposed to be doing."

The impromptu session with Maria left me feeling far more optimistic than I had in some time. It was as if you went to one doctor who told you that you have a terrible brain tumor and have only six months to live. Then you go for a second opinion and the other doctor says, "Oh, there's nothing seriously wrong with you. Just change your diet and start walking every day and you'll be fine." My brain could hardly take it in, but I sensed that the second opinion was the right one.

Darci had said you can't work for money, so I knew what *not* to work for. Maria told me I wasn't working in the correct field, and I sensed she was right, yet she did not offer a solution either. Somewhere deep inside I had known there must be another way, but I hadn't found it yet. In truth, I felt rudderless and in need of inspired leadership. The whole time I was learning to swim with the sharks, I was heavily undergunned and always looking for mentors. I had found one in William F. Buckley, whose weekly TV program, *Firing Line*, I watched religiously. It wasn't Buckley's politics that interested me as much as his mastery of speech, which provided a virtual classroom for me. I was also struck by a passage in one of his many books in which he offered the advice that if you don't know what you're doing with your life, your sole job is to sit down and not move until you figure out what you *should* be doing. I realized that I had come to just such a moment, and rather than muddle through with my current job, I needed to stop and make a course correction.

The next day I went to my office at the real estate firm and stared at my computer monitor until I arrived at a momentous decision. I closed all my files, put my calendar away, and prepared to go home. It took me a while to wrap up the loose ends, but, as I'll discuss in Part II, once you decide to act, the next steps fall into place. I tendered my resignation and left.

## Chapter 9

———————

# OUT OF THE ASHES

Native American healers . . . regard
medicine as not only a life path—in
fact that's the meaning of the word—
but also a ceremonial act. So, the ritual
behavior and the ceremony associated
with healing is a very important ele-
ment, and this is a way that intentions
are clarified, that a collective field of
intention is created, and that people are
brought together.
                    —Sylver Quevedo, M.D.

Paul Brine, who was closer to my dad's age than to mine, was
quite a Renaissance man, a world traveler, art connoisseur, philanthropist, and collector of rare books. Through his travels to
Tibet, Paul had become sympathetic to the cause of Tibetan liberation and was close with a number of Tibetan lamas. He had
begun lending financial support to an organization called Free
Tibet, which campaigns for an end to the Chinese occupation of

Tibet and includes a number of celebrities, such as Richard Gere.

One day Paul invited me to dinner to meet a couple of friends, a man and woman a few years younger than I. He occupied the penthouse of the Langham, an apartment building across Seventy-third Street from the Dakota on Central Park West. His entire apartment was stocked with artifacts from Asia and Europe—Tibetan *tankhas,* Eastern European icons, and other objects of religious art. The penthouse was painted all in white, the ceiling consisted of glass skylights, and one wall of the living room was completely covered with an elaborate Greek mosaic depicting the blinding of St. Paul on the road to Damascus.

One of his friends, named Peter, had helped install a sophisticated stereo system throughout the apartment. The speakers and other gear were concealed, but the sound was exhilarating, and the dinner was Paul's way of thanking Peter for work he couldn't have done himself. We sat looking out over Central Park through big picture windows, sipping our wine as Paul regaled us with vivid accounts of his travels to Tibet.

Taking in the splendid view as Paul went on with his travelogue, I happened to notice what appeared to be red snowflakes floating upward. I found this so odd that I got up from the table and walked over to the window. In fact, the "snowflakes" were big bits of debris, glowing like embers escaping from some huge, invisible fireplace. I called out to Paul, but he was enmeshed in his narration. "Don't interrupt me," he said. "I'm trying to tell a story!"

I moved to another window, from which I could see, to my great dismay, rolling flames pouring from the window of the apartment next door to Paul's, which happened to belong to Peter Jennings's ex-wife, Valerie. Finally I got his attention and insisted that everyone come to the windows. "The apartment next door is in flames!" I yelled, and we now saw fire engines and a hook-and-ladder pulling up outside, lights flashing, air horns blasting. Firemen were rushing into the building, so Paul announced that they looked like they had things under control and insisted we return to the dinner table. We'd all had some wine by now, and he was completely caught up in his storytelling. I walked toward the wall with the Greek mosaic, which adjoined the apartment next door, and put my hand on it. It was definitely getting hot, but before I could work up the courage to interrupt Paul again, we heard an insistent pounding on the door.

Paul opened it to find a fire chief and three firemen carrying rolls of hose over their shoulders, axes in their hands, and Scott Air-Paks on their backs for oxygen if needed. They asked if there was a fire inside, and Paul said no. Then they said they had to get to the roof terrace to gain access to the apartment next door.

"Well," Paul said with real annoyance, "you can't come through my garden terrace. In fact, you're interrupting our dinner party."

The fire chief looked at him as if he were crazy, and then at me. I shoved Paul into the hall, and like a traffic cop I pointed to the French doors leading to the terrace, on which were arrayed a wooden partition wall with ivy-covered trellises as well as an antique statue of the Buddha that Paul had brought from Tibet and a small reflecting pool. "You can get access through there," I said. "Jennings's terrace is on the other side of the trellis, and there's a ladder running up the side of a small pyramid on the roof."

The chief stepped through, talking with his men. He looked at the man with the ax. "Take that wall down," he commanded. Then, to the other two, "Stretch that hose over that pyramid!" And they were off. Paul tried to follow them onto the terrace to stop them from penetrating the trellis. But I grabbed his arm and told him to stand down. Having been in the Navy many years ago, Paul seemed to hear in the tone of my voice a little of my experience as a company commander at the maritime college.

"Paul," I said. "Stop, really! You could get arrested for interfering."

When the man with the ax succeeded in knocking down the trellis, I saw that the ceiling of the Jennings apartment was ablaze, as if there were a rolling ocean of flame on its surface. And as they broke out the windows, the waves of flames did not pass through the windows but instead rolled off the ceiling and began to climb the walls like a living thing. The hoses were charged, the nozzle switch thrown back, and a powerful stream began dousing the flames. The firemen never told us to leave but just kept working.

After ten minutes the fire was extinguished, and an hour later they had coiled their hoses and were gone. The chief came back inside Paul's apartment, walked over to the common wall where the massive mosaic hung, placed his palm on the white paint, and felt it. "Hmm, still very warm," he said. "You're lucky the fire didn't pass this point."

Our host made a joke about St. Paul saving us. We had finished the cold poached salmon and had some more wine when suddenly Paul started sobbing. He explained that the following week a number of Tibetan monks and lamas and their supporters would be holding a demonstration at the United Nations building and having a fund-raising dinner. Paul had invited a small contingent, including the Dalai Lama and Richard Gere, to sit in his penthouse garden with the reflecting pool and statue of the Buddha, surrounded by the trellises with their English ivy. But now the trellises and the partition that held them up were smashed to bits.

As he talked about his disappointment and wept, my heart went out to him. "Listen, Paul," I said, "I can help you. I have been working with wood with my dad since I was a child. And I have the tools. If I can build a boat, I'm sure I can rebuild the trellises from photos you have of them. I'll have this all rebuilt by next week." Paul thought it was impossible, but I convinced him otherwise. We ordered everything that would be needed, and the next day I went to work, reconstructing the partition wall and rebuilding the trellises and reflecting pool. The ivy itself hadn't been seriously harmed, so we just led what remained to the new trellis and wove it by hand through the latticework.

Paul was overcome with gratitude, and as a reward he invited me to the private reception for the Tibetans. Although I had met Paul in the context of business and materialism, he was one of the few deeply spiritual people I knew. I hadn't been aware of this other level of his personality, however, so when he asked me one day if I prayed, the question caught me completely off guard. I fudged some kind of answer, but it was clear that I didn't consider prayer of much value. Paul put his hand on my shoulder and looked me in the eye. Although he was in his seventies, his hand was surprisingly firm. On the wall of his penthouse garden I had seen an old pair of oars, mementos of his days on the Yale crew, and he still had that kind of wiry strength. As he spoke now, he increased the pressure of his hand on my shoulder and looked me directly in the eye. "You have to pray," he said intently. It was one of the few times he had ever spoken to me in such a direct way.

So I saw this chance to meet these highly evolved lamas as a natural progression in my spiritual education. At the gathering, Paul introduced me to many of the monks and lamas, and especially to the physician for the Dalai Lama. Paul told the physician that I was interested in healing and meditation. The physician said that for hundreds of years in Tibet they had studied the connection between meditation, spiritual practice, and healing. He told me that many Tibetan physicians had learned how to bring their consciousness to bear on broken bones and vibrate the internal structure of the bones as if they could realign the very molecules.

I could hardly believe what I was hearing. I asked him if he could do such things. Unfortunately, he said, he couldn't, nor could his teacher, although his teacher had told him that *his* teacher could. Somewhere along the way the sacred knowledge was lost. It wasn't clear to me what had caused this loss. The invasion by the Chinese army in 1950, their attacks on spirituality in their agenda to forcibly modernize the Tibetans, and the destruction of many ancient texts certainly hadn't helped matters.

One thing I did know was that this capability was undreamed of by Western medicine; it was certainly worthy of exploration. This thought sparked a sudden recall of some ads my dad had made after he was replaced as the Marlboro Man. He was reincarnated as the Kellogg's Corn Flakes Cowboy, depicted dressed in a denim jacket and Stetson hat and sitting at a lunch counter a few stools away from an attractive woman in modern business attire. The ad copy went, "East is east and west is west and never the twain shall meet, except maybe over a bowl of Kellogg's Corn Flakes." What, I mused, if the spiritual practices alive in the East were married to the science and technology of the West?

When I was growing up, I had been taught that we are all children of God, that we are imbued with a sacred inheritance. But what if our sacred inheritance includes the ability to heal other people by opening our hearts, making it our heart's desire to provide our suffering fellow beings with tangible benefits?

One other event at that gathering strengthened my sense of being among people who experienced the world with a sense of sacred potential that was different from most of the people I had ever known. As I was standing by myself in the foyer, Paul came over and grabbed me by the elbow. "Come," he said, "I will introduce you now." He indicated a senior monk who was clearly the center of attention. "I told them that it was you who rebuilt the trellises and the reflecting pool." But I suddenly acted like a stubborn mule, refusing to be dragged over to meet the Tibetan holy man. As I took in that scene, the senior monk turned his head toward me. Our eyes met, I smiled and nodded at him, and he nodded back at me. I was silently sending him the message that I wouldn't burden him with the chatter of one more mouth, and he appeared to smile as if in receipt of my thought. As the monk was leaving an hour or so later, Paul introduced me to him. Again, he simply smiled and nodded, but then someone whisked him away. A few moments later, another monk approached and asked me to step into Paul's library. There the senior monk was standing, and he finally spoke to me. "I wanted to thank you personally for repairing the terrace—we are enjoying the peace here," he said. Then he added politely, "Who are you?"

At a reception that included world dignitaries, United Nations representatives, university professors, and holy men, I hardly stood out. "Oh," I said smiling, "I'm nobody." His own smile broadened, but he also looked quite serious, if it's possible to look serious while laughing. "No," he said, "you're not nobody."

Then he took the silk scarf from around his neck and draped it about mine. He looked at me and smiled as if wishing me the peace emanating from his heart. I was tongue-tied, not knowing what was appropriate to say or do. He made a little sign over the center of his chest. "I just wanted to return the blessing that you shared with me before," he said in surprisingly good English.

I did my best to reciprocate the gesture and the smile as some other monks came and led him away. In that moment, I knew that he had received my silent message. It may seem like a small thing, but a lot can be communicated by a glance if we're attentive. And that exchange was another confirmation of the profound nature of our sacred capacity. These monks spent hours each day in meditation, prayer, prostrations, and other spiritual practices. Together, these amounted to a purification or centering that clearly helped them to focus their spiritual energies, heightening their awareness of their sacred inheritance and allowing them to communicate with uncommon levels of intimacy.

In the Tibetan tradition, I later learned, offering a white silk scarf called a *khata* is an expression of auspicious intentions at the beginning of a relationship. You can offer a khata as a blessing on any new relationship, from marriage to a business or political partnership, and it recognizes a moment of powerful change and transition in your life. The white silk scarf announces that the giver's intentions are positive and pure, and that it is a genuine blessing from the heart. In this case, I'm sure, it symbolized my growing involvement with spirit, with teachers and healers from many traditions. Without even being fully aware of it, I received a blessing from this Tibetan holy man after our shared moment of empathy—a blessing that helped to galvanize my progress on the path of exploration I had recently begun.

When a fire burns away part of a thick forest, consuming both the trees and the weeds that are choking the ground, we sometimes think of it as a great loss. What was once a woodland filled with life is suddenly reduced to a charred, acrid-smelling rubble. But in reality, that cleansing fire clears away the old growth, and activates seeds that have lain dormant in the ground.

If the apartment next to Paul's hadn't caught fire and caused his terrace garden to be destroyed, and if I hadn't been moved in my heart to help rebuild it, I might not have met that Tibetan physician who planted for me the seeds of the possibility of healing beyond the bounds of conventional medicine. Whether I knew it or not, the white silk khata represented a blessing that moved me to the next step on my journey of discovery.

My encounter with the Tibetan doctor was, in reality, the third leg of a stool that I had been unconsciously constructing. Sometime before that meeting, a good friend had provided me with

an introduction to Dr. Patricia Carrington, a psychology professor at Princeton with a great interest in meditation. They say the
longest distance you can traverse is not from one continent to
another but from your left ear to your right ear. I had explored
the exterior world. I had sailed across good portions of the globe
during my education at the maritime college. I had been in the
Rainbow Room with Tony Bennett. But I hadn't yet done any
interior exploration. So, within a week I was on a bus to Princeton, New Jersey, to study meditation with a woman I'd never
met, who had agreed to teach me privately as a favor to a family friend.

I could hardly have found a more accomplished teacher. Among
other things, Patricia is the originator of Clinically Standardized
Meditation, a training method used in medical institutions and
other organizations for stress reduction and a host of medical and
psychological conditions. I liked Patricia, who was kind and not
pretentious at all. Her instructions were clear as could be, and
she started me on a sort of secular meditation practice that didn't
involve any religious jargon and that made me more comfortable
with the process. I worked with Patricia for a while and practiced
on my own to learn to still my mind.

In the months that followed, I began to explore tai chi chuan
(also called taiji). My teacher, C. K. Chu, was a tremendous gift
on my journey. Born in Hong Kong, Chu began his martial arts
training at age twelve and has taught tai chi and internal Chinese
disciplines such as nei kung for over thirty years, as well as author-
ing several books. Combined with a master's degree in physics
and teaching experience at the university level, he possessed the
capacity to convey the principles of Chinese internal disciplines
in terms of Western scientific and philosophical concepts. Chu
said, "My philosophy of physical and mental development can be
reduced to the basic Taoist principle 'Go with nature and improve

what you have.' Within these simple words lie the secrets with which one can restructure the mind and body."

If the first leg of my stool consisted of the Hindu concepts that Dr. Carrington conveyed in meditation, Chu's insight provided the second leg. When I started training with him, I told him that I had already had some training in meditation. "A path," Chu said, "is made with the footsteps of many people." Nei kung dates to the beginning of Chinese history, in the third millennium B.C.E. For thousands of years these esoteric disciplines remained confined to a relatively small group of teachers and their students. These secrets were transmitted from teacher to student over the centuries, and I was fortunate to find Mr. Chu as a teacher.

The third leg of my spiritual stool, then, came from the Tibetan physician I met at Paul's reception. He had made a kind of syllogistic analogy: In Tibet,

A. the doctors could focus their minds through spiritual practice
B. they could develop mastery over the flow of consciousness, or life force so
C. they could focus their life force to effect physical healing.

When Paul Brine retired to the island of St. Barts, he bequeathed to me his collection of books on sacred teachings from the world's great traditions. As I delved into them, filled with gratitude for this wondrous gift, I found a similar thread running through all the books, namely, that we each possess a sacred potential. And if we cultivate this inheritance by raising our consciousness, it will allow us to manifest physical changes in the world. I had also read teachings distilled by Deepak Chopra from his knowledge of both ancient Ayurvedic wisdom and modern medical science, each of which shows in different ways that we are vibrating molecular beings whose entire physical composition changes every seven years. So maybe I didn't resonate with the catalogs of the medical schools that I had previously ordered while searching for a new career because they were based on a materialist worldview.

Yet, even though the seeds had been planted, meditation, my nei kung teacher, and the Tibetan physician could not show me how to manifest physical change as it was represented in so many sacred texts from the Hindu, Taoist, Tibetan, Jewish, and Christian traditions. I would keep searching, but my sacred potential would not be ignited until that night in my basement studio when I dreamed with the imagination of a child and felt the joy of what it would be like to physically heal another human being.

# Chapter 10

BUILDING THE BRIDGE

> The essence of the crisis presenting
> humanity is that we are approaching
> the limits of our knowledge . . . and we
> are now in need of turning our atten-
> tion to the consciousness of ourselves.
>
> —Jonas Salk

The transformation that began in my basement workshop at the dawn of the new millennium, as I described in Chapter 2, was not unique to me. Indeed, it fits into a pattern that has been observed and written about by a number of scientists, researchers, journalists, and other observers. Although their many books and articles haven't all entered the realm of household knowledge, you could say that the world is nearing the tipping point of discovering and accepting them. When that happens, as I believe it must, it will have enormous consequences for all of us.

One sign that this process is already under way is that enormously popular films, television programs, and books, including Dan Brown's bestselling novel *The Lost Symbol,* have incorporated many of these new perceptions in a fictional context. Yet even a number of nonfiction works in this field have begun to attract a following. A simple example of how the work of these visionary scientists and researchers corresponds to my own experience is a book such as *The Sense of Being Stared At, and Other Aspects of the Extended Mind*, by the Cambridge- and Harvard-trained scientist Rupert Sheldrake. Relying primarily on hard scientific data, peer-reviewed studies, and his own extensive research, Sheldrake shows that "telepathy, the sense of being stared at, and precognition occur both in nonhuman animals, such as cats and dogs, and in people. They are not 'paranormal' or 'supernatural.' They are normal and natural, part of our biological nature."

Sheldrake's work explains the experience I had on the beach at Smith Point Park, when I felt inexplicably called to head out into the fog, not realizing that the call was coming from a couple of people in danger of losing their vehicle to the sea. Despite the growing body of scientific evidence to support it, the concept of communicating in nontraditional ways still brings cynical responses from many people, who are heavily invested in the mechanistic worldview. But, as Sheldrake points out, to an eighteenth-century physicist, "Seeing things at a distance or hearing the voices of people far away would have seemed like the work of witches or the delusions of lunatics. Now they are everyday experiences, thanks to television, radio, and telephones."

Sheldrake's findings happen to fit into an even broader category of astonishing conceptions backed up by hard science, particularly in the field known as quantum physics. We could easily spend the rest of this book exploring the ramifications of all the exciting discoveries in quantum physics since Max Planck introduced this paradigm-busting concept early in the twentieth century, for which he won the Nobel Prize in Physics. Planck's premise that the observer affects what is observed was relegated to the back pages of newspapers in his day, but, fortunately, a number of contemporary researchers and journalists have expertly summarized the work of Planck, Niels Bohr, and their many followers in a way that is clear and accessible. One of the most significant principles of this research is that the observer affects the person or object being observed.

Dr. Patricia Muehsam is the founder of the first national initiative in curriculum development in alternative and complementary medicine, at the Association of American Medical Colleges, and has directed laboratory research investigating mind-matter and mind-body interactions. She has pointed out that "researchers in physics and engineering labs have been conducting experiments that suggest the profound effect of consciousness on the material world: how our thoughts can affect us, literally, and physically. For over twenty-five years, scientists at Princeton University's Princeton Engineering Anomalies Research (PEAR) Laboratory have demonstrated powerful correlations between human intention and machine behavior. They have shown that untrained individuals can influence the output of random mechanical and electronic number generators, just by thinking in which direction the numbers should go. These effects were found to be independent of space and time. Effects also occurred when the individual was thousands of miles away."

For that to be possible, some sort of unmeasurable ability to communicate between objects must exist. All the great spiritual paths have been teaching us for centuries that all life is connected in such a way that what happens to other beings affects each of us, whether or not we recognize it. In the words attributed to the Native American Chief Seattle, "What we do to the web, we do to all of us." That connectedness is at the heart of the Buddha's teaching that to think of ourselves as separate beings is an illusion that leads to the poisons of greed, hatred, and ignorance. It is even implicit in the age-old teachings espoused in nearly identical language by Confucius, Jesus, and Rabbi Hillel: "Do to others as you would have them do to you." Before now, these teachings were thought of as religious or ethical ideals, but few people believed that it is literally true that we are all connected. Now science is increasingly pointing in that direction.

The award-winning journalist Lynne McTaggart has interviewed many of the leading minds in this new field and has reported on their work in great detail in her books *The Field* and *The Intention Experiment*. Of one of the key discoveries of researchers in this arena, she has written, "They had demonstrated that big things like atoms were nonlocally connected, even in matter so large that you could hold it in your hand." As the title of her book *The Field* suggests, a vast web of connectedness links not only human beings but all matter. Some spiritual teachers have referred to this concept as the Divine Matrix.

Other spiritual teachings and mystical practices have increasingly been shown to have practical counterparts in the material world. For millennia, masters of Western, Eastern, and indigenous spiritual traditions have taught the immense potential of meditation and prayer for developing our spiritual consciousness. Now, at the most basic level, we have learned that meditation can help us physically by reducing stress and even lowering blood pressure. This tangible link between consciousness and physical reality has been scientifically documented by highly respected physicians and researchers, such as Herbert Benson of the Harvard Medical School. Benson's *Relaxation Response*, based on thousand-year-old principles of meditation and first published in 1975, is now widely used in hospitals and private practice to help prevent strokes, heart attacks, and depression.

William Tiller, a professor at Stanford University, is the author of *Conscious Acts of Creation: The Emergence of a New Physics,* in which he explains the results of his research on how human intention alters material properties and chemical reactions. Tiller's work mines the same veins as McTaggart, Sheldrake, and popular authors and teachers including Gregg Braden and Caroline Myss. He argues for a new understanding of physics, one that disproves the paradigm—based on three-hundred-year-old scientific theory—that human intention has no influence on material properties. The old paradigm, developed by scientists beginning with Isaac Newton and Charles Darwin, was the product of the so-called Age of Reason. Their ideas were revolutionary then, providing a much-needed remedy to the superstition and ignorance of the Dark Ages and the unquestioned power of the church. But that paradigm is being replaced by a new worldview. As Rupert Sheldrake observes, "The boundaries of the 'normal' are not fixed, but shift according to changes in scientific orthodoxies." For the last few centuries, matter had been viewed as the fundamental reality, he points out, but today "fields" and "energy" are considered more fundamental. "The boundaries of scientific 'normality' are shifting again with a dawning recognition of the reality of consciousness. The powers of the mind, hitherto ignored by physics, are the new scientific frontier."

Indeed, before the advent of the microscope, doctors weren't aware that they were transmitting disease from patient to patient by not washing their hands or sanitizing their instruments, simply because the deadly microbes were invisible to the unaided eye. Dr. Tiller's findings, for example, suggest that human intention has enormous influence on our environment. His experiments and those that McTaggart and others have been writing about seek to render obsolete the Newtonian idea that we are all separate individuals, connected only marginally by familial, national, religious, and ethnic links. McTaggart says instead that "at our essence we exist as a unity, a relationship—utterly interdependent, the parts affecting the whole at every moment." This is remarkably similar to the teachings of contemporary spiritual masters such as Thich Nhat Hanh, the Vietnamese Buddhist monk, who says, "We are all Related. We interare."

This redefining of who we are and how we interact with other people will turn out to be the most crucial development of the twenty-first century. Yet even the scientists and researchers whose studies have paved the way for the new paradigm are still looking for convincing proof on a larger, more tangible scale. In his book *The Divine Matrix*, Gregg Braden writes, "On the smallest level of the universe, atoms and subatomic particles do in fact act as if they're connected. The problem is that scientists don't know how or even if the behavior observed on such tiny scales has any meaning for the larger realities of our daily lives."

We already know that mammals of the sky and sea can emit waves that allow them to navigate in the dark. We've learned from studying bats how to mimic the mechanism they use, leading to the development of radar. Whales and dolphins also navigate and communicate by emitting waves, and we have learned to use sonar (an acronym for sound navigation ranging) to safely travel the fog-shrouded seas, day and night, on the surface and below the water. Healthcare is also evolving to integrating these discoveries in noninvasive ways. Physicians now use wave technology to penetrate patients' bodies from a distance and dissolve kidney stones (a procedure called lithotripsy), whereas just a few years ago surgeons needed to cut open the patient to gain access to the kidneys. So it's hardly a stretch to talk about learning to project our thoughts into the world, not only to communicate but also to affect matter on a large scale. We now know that thoughts are measurable things that extend beyond our bodies. At the end of *The Lost Symbol*, Dan Brown writes, "Within a matter of years modern man will be forced to accept what is now unthinkable:

our minds can generate energy capable of transforming physical matter."

Brown's book is only fiction, of course, yet he acknowledges basing the characters who say these lines on real people, including Lynne McTaggart and Marilyn M. Schlitz, director of research at the Institute of Noetic Sciences. That organization, founded by the *Apollo 14* astronaut Edgar Mitchell after he had walked on the moon, is dedicated to carrying out cutting-edge research into the potential of consciousness. Consciousness is beginning to be seen as having dominion over the world. It has always been so, of course; we just haven't recognized it. The great statesmen who signed the Declaration of Independence were able to stand up to the mightiest military force on earth and give birth to a nation based on the power of a new paradigm—one in which the highest good was perceived to be not military force and financial wealth but life, liberty, and the pursuit of happiness. Mahatma Gandhi, with steadfast belief in his own consciousness and the power of nonviolent resistance, was able to evict an occupying army from his homeland. Anything is indeed possible.

I had discovered for myself that anything is possible after my initial experience in my basement studio led to the series of spontaneous healings I described in Chapter 5. As those healings continued, I decided to seek out advice from medical professionals, lawyers, and even a seasoned news reporter. They all seemed to agree on one thing: If I wanted to change the status quo, I would need to find some way of documenting the work I was doing. It was like the proverbial question: If a tree falls in the forest and nobody hears it, did it make a sound? I was led to understand that, no matter how impressive a healing might seem to the person receiving it, unless I could produce before and after medical records verifying significant results, the testimony of medical doctors, as well as documented accounts from the recipients expressing precisely what they had experienced, it would be as if nothing had happened. So, as the next step toward manifesting my dream of helping people, I set about creating a mechanism to document and archive everything I was doing, resulting in empirical evidence from a series of observational studies that I will detail in the next chapter.

# Chapter 11

## BODY OF EVIDENCE

All great truths begin as heresy.
—Aldous Huxley
(quoted in R. D. Lamm,
*"The Great Heretics"*)

The most heretical evidence of all concerned the role of
consciousness. . . . Directing thoughts at a target seemed
capable of altering machines, cells, and, indeed, entire
multicelled organisms like human beings.
—Lynne McTaggart

As I observed Joseph work, through my scientific, clinical
eyes, my perception permanently shifted. I witnessed the
effective intervention of a modality not known by Western medicine. Joseph was transforming human tissue,
through intention, within a matter of minutes.
—Frank Salvatore, M.D.

After I discovered that we have the potential to transform human
tissue, I knew that the concept I was presenting not only was

heretical but also ran in direct opposition to some strongly held beliefs of mainstream science and medicine. The physicians who broke ranks to advise me cautioned that the concept was not in accord with the teachings of science and, further, the pendulum had swung so far that science had effectively relegated the concept to myth.

I knew I had my work cut out for me, but I was not going to shy away from exploration of the truth. I decided to treat the discovery as an opportunity and a challenge, and I began to plan how best to prepare a plausible case to support it. I took stock of the situation and considered my qualifications. I realized that four years at the State University of New York pursuing a bachelor of science degree, studying admiralty law and physics, and taking a few engineering classes was inadequate to equip me to explain or understand the mechanism behind the healings that were being replicated daily in my office. Later, as it became evident that my soul was more like that of a monk than like that of a warrior, I entered an interfaith seminary and studied world religion, but reading the sacred texts of the major religions also did not equip me to understand how I was altering human tissue. I arrived at the conclusion that neither science nor religion had a monopoly on the truth. Einstein seemed to agree; he had voiced his opinion that there existed opportunity for further understanding when he said, "Science without religion is lame. Religion without science is blind."

One of my first mentors instilled in me the importance of recording the results of my work on people and archiving the empirical data that was generated. Having made the decision to adhere to this rule, I began to seek out a team of professionals to assist me. I would need a seasoned filmmaker with experience in the medical world to document the effects of a modality not currently taught or reported in any medical journal. I found that person in Marc Wishengrad, an award-winning filmmaker who had been nominated for an Emmy for his cinematography on Discovery Communications's *Trauma: Life in the E.R.* and regularly shoots for C-SPAN. In addition, Marc has worked for years at New York–Presbyterian Hospital and has captured new surgical procedures for the renowned cardiothoracic surgeon Dr. Mehmet Oz. Marc was the perfect person for the assignment; not only is he a world-recognized professional in medical cinematography but he also comes from a journalistic lineage.

Marc explained how he would go about documenting the work. We drafted an agreement for his fee, his team's camera equipment, truck, lighting and sound equipment. There was, however, one aspect that I had not anticipated. Marc explained to me that he had a reputation to maintain, so I would need to hire an experienced journalist to interview the doctors and people participating in an unbiased, professional manner. The very next evening an attorney friend of mine, Anthony Occocio, invited me to a reception he was hosting at a New York City hotel. There I was introduced to Christy Musumeci. She told me that she had worked as a television news reporter down South but had relocated to New York City to try to make it on the national level. Christy already had a foot in the door, having landed a position with MSNBC, and she would soon realize her professional dream of becoming a prime-time national news anchor.

I explained my plan to film a short documentary exploring whether it was possible for a human being to direct consciousness with enough precision to achieve physical change in tissue and bone. She waited for the punch line, and stared at me unflinchingly, but none came. I asked Christy if she could recommend any intern television journalists I could hire for a reasonable fee. She looked at me as if peering into my soul. Then she told me that her brother was a medical doctor in Massachusetts who specialized in pain management. Pain is difficult to see or measure, she said, but it is very real indeed, so she thought the subject I was exploring was intriguing.

"When is your shoot date?" she asked. I told her it was the following Thursday. "Hmm," Christy said. "That happens to be my day off. I'll do it for you. I'd be interested in interviewing these doctors and getting their firsthand accounts." I told her that we had limited resources. "I'll do it for free," she said.

I could barely believe how everything was coming together; it was as if the universe was conspiring to make this documentary a reality. "But you need to know how I work," she added. "I'm a professional journalist, and I will ask objective questions." Apparently the jury was still out with her too, and she was sharp as a tack. I liked her immediately.

That fit perfectly with what Marc wanted to do, so together the camera crew and the reporter set out to record the testimonies of doctors and ordinary people. Along with Marc and Christy's interviews, we archived relevant medical records and professional transcripts. Based on those records and follow-up MRIs, which would arrive later, we were able to give accurate accounts of many of the original cases. Three of those case studies make up the balance of this chapter.

## Case 1. Swollen Knee

> What was unusual was what he did, to watch my
> knee transform.
> —Elizabeth Muss, M.D.

At the beginning, most people who came to see me had learned about my work from someone I had helped or from a friend or relative of someone I had helped. Most of them were ordinary folks with no connection to the world of science or conventional medicine. But one day in 2000, I got a call from Elizabeth Muss. "I've heard about what you've been doing," she said, "and I believe some of these things are possible." I asked her what she did, and she revealed that she was a medical doctor, a cardiologist in private practice in the Bristol Medical Building in Manhattan and affiliated with a prominent East Side hospital. She said that she was open to combining conventional medical techniques with some integrative therapies. She was "always looking for other ways to do things" and wanted to experience firsthand how I worked. As she later put it, "I decided that I would be my own guinea pig. I would see how it went so that I could refer patients if it seemed to be a modality that worked. And it does."

Dr. Muss wanted to see if I could help her with what she described as "a serious problem" with her knee, which she had injured long ago. "This has been a chronic problem for years," she said. Moreover, she had recently twisted her ankle, and the physical therapy for the ankle had exacerbated the problem with her knee. She was scheduled to have more physical therapy, but her husband had met someone who knew me and suggested she call.

I was exhilarated at the opportunity to work with a medical doctor, who would bring her trained eye and observational skills to bear. When Dr. Muss arrived at my office, I saw a professional, rather fit-looking woman about fifty years of age in a business suit and skirt. Sitting up on my table, she gave me the history of her knee injury in detailed medical terminology. After describing the injury, she said, "Let me show you."

Dr. Muss elevated the hem of her skirt just enough to permit me to see both knees. One of her knees looked perfectly normal, with the patella—kneecap—cleanly articulated. Her other knee, however, was obviously swollen. For a moment, as I compared the two knees side by side, I was reminded of the two church carvings I had been given to restore, one in relatively good shape and the other clearly disfigured. The swelling in her right knee was so pronounced that I couldn't make out the shape of her kneecap. She asked me what I thought. "I think the knee can be healed," I said. I requested that she recline and just relax as I began the process.

But Dr. Muss sat up on the table, saying that she wanted to watch while I worked on her. Most people came just to receive the result and didn't care to observe, but given her career, I understood and appreciated her professional interest. I told her to observe closely what was happening during the process. As I focused my awareness on her injured knee, the swelling began to break down. Within a couple of minutes, the shape of her knee began to emerge. "Wow!" Dr. Muss said. "That's amazing! How are you doing that?"

She described in detail what she was witnessing, her medically trained eyes adept at objectively recording the tangible changes, and she wanted an explanation from me.

"I can't really explain it in scientific terms," I said. "Each day, I gain a greater understanding of the process."

Later, on camera, Christy began to interview Dr. Muss, asking her to describe what had happened that day in my office, and the doctor was very plain about it. "What was unusual was what he did," she said, "to watch my knee transform, to watch the skin pucker."

After we worked together that first day, Dr. Muss got off the table and tested the injured knee. She told me that she was able to bend it deeply in a way she hadn't been able to do in a long time. "My God," she said, "the knee you worked on feels stronger than my other knee now." When interviewed later, Dr. Muss reported that her athletic abilities had returned to levels she had enjoyed prior to her injury. "I've regained my strength, and I can now bend deep into the knee," she said.


## Case 2. Fractured Arm

> He looks at me, looks at my rotation, and says, "This is miraculous. And by the way, you don't need any physical therapy."
> —Greg Sherman

In August 2008, Greg Sherman went to enter a cab in Upper Manhattan and instead fell into a large pothole, landing sharply on his right arm. "There's a kind of shock that goes through the body," he said when asked to describe what he felt at that moment. "It's different than pain initially. It's a trauma, but you know that your body is really badly damaged and there's a real problem." It was after ten o'clock at night, so Greg decided to wait till the next day to seek medical help, but the pain became unbearable. "It went to the maximum threshold I've ever felt in my life," he said.

After Greg arrived at Mount Sinai's emergency room at six o'clock the following morning, he was put on intravenous Valium and his arm was given a series of X-rays, which revealed a Monteggia fracture. Named for the surgeon who first described it, this complex fracture comprises a multiple break of the ulna that affects the joint with the radius—the two parallel bones that make up the forearm. In Greg's case the fracture was also comminuted, which meant that the bone had been broken into a number of pieces. Because the elbow joint is affected, a Monteggia fracture can be difficult to heal properly, and the first surgeon Greg consulted recommended surgery to implant a metal plate and screws to stabilize the bones. The surgeon informed Greg that even with the surgery, however, the best-case scenario was that he would not be able to use his arm actively for six to eight weeks and would never regain full extension or range of motion.

The surgeon recommended that Greg have the surgery in a couple of days. He added that Greg would require full anesthesia and considerable recovery time. Greg asked when the plate and screws would come out, and the surgeon informed him that they had to stay in forever. Understandably, Greg was hesitant to have such an operation and still end up with limited range of motion. He had also read about how long it can take for the body to recover completely from full anesthesia. "I asked if they could do a local anesthesia," he said later, "but they didn't want to, because they were afraid of my arm moving during surgery. I told them I wasn't ready for major surgery and needed a few more days to think about it."

Greg went for a second opinion to a surgeon at NYU Medical Center who had treated his brother after a nasty fall some years before. The second surgeon concurred with the first surgeon's diagnosis. Finally, Greg went for a third opinion to a surgeon at the Columbia University Medical Center who had been strongly recommended by a colleague. This surgeon also suggested surgery, stating that "this is a highly unstable type of fracture and one which usually would be treated with a plate and screws in order to line it up and hold it that way." The surgeon noted that Greg was scheduled for surgery in two days, and he considered that appropriate. So Greg resigned himself to having the operation performed at Mount Sinai. He had the necessary blood work done and prepared for the inevitable.

I had known Greg as a successful executive with a background in engineering who owned several businesses and directed a business conference center that hosted events for top pharmaceutical companies. He had been kind enough to agree to host a screening there of the documentary footage we had captured to date. When I arrived one day to meet with Greg, accompanied by a medical doctor with whom I was documenting my work, I saw that Greg's arm was in a sling and asked him what had happened. He explained about the accident and the surgeons' recommendations. He had his X-rays with him, so the doctor threw them up on a light table used for viewing slides and transparencies and confirmed the multiple fracture. As often happens when people with health challenges are around me, Greg asked if I would help him. I said that I believed his bones could heal quickly. In short, I said yes, I would help. With the doctor observing, I worked on Greg right there, and the next day he reported that his arm was virtually painless, the swelling had all but disappeared, and the bruising was gone.

"I now had three professional opinions," Greg said when Marc Wishengrad documented his case in November 2008. "And they all agreed that my course of action should be surgery, and promptly." That was when he encountered me. "Right now," Greg continued, "as you can see, I have pretty much full extension. I have almost full rotation, and there's nothing left but a little bit of trauma in this arm."

A few weeks before our taping, Greg had decided to have a follow-up examination at the Hospital for Special Surgery, one of the premier institutions in the country for the treatment of musculoskeletal injuries. He saw a specialist in injuries concerning the hands, shoulders, and elbows. "He looked at my X-rays," Greg added, "and he said, 'You're doing very well. Most people would get plates and screws to guarantee outcome. You're very lucky.'"

The surgeon recommended a protective arm wrap like the ones used by skateboarders to prevent re-injury. He also recommended that Greg see a physical therapist as a precaution. "I went to one physical therapy session," Greg said. "He looks at me, looks at my rotation, and says, 'This is miraculous. And by the way, you don't need any physical therapy. There's no charge for today.'"

The following May, Greg went for evaluation to yet another surgeon at the Hospital for Special Surgery, who took follow-up X-rays of his arm and made a written report. It reads in part, "There has been complete interval healing of the mildly comminuted fracture deformity of the proximal ulna as well as the obliquely oriented intra-articular fracture of the radial head. Radiocapitellar joint alignment is satisfactory. No acute osseous abnormalities are seen." In layman's terms, the fractured bone and the damage to the elbow joint were both fully healed, and the bones were properly aligned.

Greg asked to add a few words at the end of the tape. "This really needs to be supported," he said of the outcome study he had taken part in. "This shouldn't just be for me. This needs to be for everyone. And if it was researched properly, it could really spread out . . . fairly quickly. But I think it needs to be researched immediately. It needs to be documented, it needs to be taught. It's important that this immediately gets funded. Because when my son falls or has his accident, I wouldn't want him to have plates and screws. I'd want him to benefit from this approach."

## Case 3. Inoperable Brain Tumor

> MRI scan of the brain from 4-12-02 was compared to today's scan and shows a significant improvement with less enhancement.

You will recall that early in my career I worked with a man named Gene, whose wife, Louise, brought him to my office in Manhattan all the way from Arlington, Virginia (as described in Chapter 5). Gene had been suffering from an inoperable brain tumor and was in severe pain because he had become habituated to his pain medication. He was in a wheelchair, unable to walk or speak. After spending a half hour with Gene, I felt large amounts of heat emanating from his head in the area where his tumor had been located. Although his appearance changed only modestly while he was in my office, his wife called ten days later to tell me that he was out of his wheelchair, walking with the help of a cane, and "talking up a storm," as she put it.

I spoke briefly with Gene that day and was excited to hear his lively voice at the other end of the phone line. He had not been able to get the follow-up MRI I had asked his wife to provide, however. Although his doctor was surprised to see Gene up and about, the hospital considered him no longer their patient, so they had "no protocol" for ordering further tests. Gene decided to offer to pay for the MRI himself, and the hospital acquiesced with his wishes. In June 2002, I received a letter from Louise with a medical report from the National Cancer Institute dated May 24, 2002, based on the most recent MRI. A yellow Post-it note attached read simply, "JP, Finally the report came in. Best, Louise."

Under "History," the report read, "Currently the patient seems to be stable overall. He walks with a cane at home now." Under "Impression," the oncologist had written, "Patient's MRI scan of the brain from 4-12-02 was compared to today's scan and shows a significant improvement with less enhancement and edema." He went on to surmise the cause for the significant improvement. "I believe that this is most likely necrosis from treatment effect."

*Necrosis* is death of the cancerous cells, resulting in the tumor shrinking. Several weeks later I received a call from Louise offering an update. She told me that Gene was at the National Rehabilitation Hospital in Washington, D.C., receiving physical therapy. "His mental state has improved," she said. "He's getting stronger every day."

So, how was all of this happening? As I described in the previous chapter, pioneers in quantum physics have clearly established a powerful relationship between human consciousness and matter. At the time I worked on Dr. Muss and others, I was hardly aware of the complexity of this relationship in a way I could articulate.

As the archiving of our work continued over the next seven years, Marc Wishengrad, together with Alison Draper, a former advertising executive whose father was a medical doctor, would interview a number of other pioneers who were committed to advancing the integration of medicine through rigorous scientific study. Marc and Alison interviewed Frank Salvatore, the board-certified surgeon who wrote the preface to this book, and Beverly Rubik, Ph.D., who is part of a new breed of scientists assisting in bridging the divide separating body, mind, and spirit. Their aim is to birth an integrative health model that holds the potential for better patient outcomes across a wide spectrum of health concerns. A biophysicist by training, Dr. Rubik helped conduct scientific research and education in the fields of mind-body, subtle energies, and complementary medicine. She has served on the Program Advisory Council to the Office of Alternative Medicine at the National Institutes of Health and conducted NIH-sponsored research on healing. In addition, in 1994, Dr. Rubik was instrumental in naming the Biofield, a matrix of energies that extend outward from each person's body.

Perhaps one of the most inspiring experts in integrative medicine whom Marc and Alison interviewed is the visionary James S. Gordon. A Harvard-trained physician who served as chairman of the White House Commission on Complementary and Alternative Medicine Policy, Dr. Gordon also founded the Center for Mind-Body Medicine in Washington, D.C. He is a world-recognized expert in using integrative techniques to heal depression, anxiety, and psychological trauma, and has long been a supporter of noninvasive modalities. "Hippocrates said, 'First, do no harm,'" Dr. Gordon said in one interview. "So it always makes sense to begin with those approaches, like mind-body approaches, which are least likely to do harm."

In his groundbreaking book *Manifesto for a New Medicine*, Gordon makes the case that recent scientific studies on the effects of distant healing and intercessory prayer, for example, have renewed interest in the healing potential described in the scriptures of the world's spiritual traditions. "They suggest," Gordon writes, "that the healing in which Jesus instructed his disciples might still be, 2000 years later, a vital component of healthcare. There is a vast literature, some of it as high quality as any medical paper, that shows that we can, simply by intending to do so, make significant positive changes in the well-being of others and in nonhuman biological systems."

His remarks correspond closely to those of the researchers and reporters I quoted in the previous chapter. But Gordon goes on to say something I find vitally important. "It would appear that both men and women who are known for their healing powers, as well as perfectly ordinary people, are capable of accomplishing this. All of these studies, which are largely unknown to or ignored by mainstream medicine, have quite extraordinary implications for health and healing, as well as for our understanding of what it means to be human."

Gordon concludes, "The research evidence is there. The change in consciousness still needs to happen." Or, as Larry Dossey writes in *Reinventing Medicine*, "In a sense, medicine is burning, as old ideas and methods are fading on every hand. But medicine's fires are purifying: new life is emerging from the ashes, as it always does. The reinventors are stepping forward, and healing is in the wind. The rebirth has begun."

## Chapter 12

---

# A SECOND OPINION

There are more things in heaven and
earth, Horatio,
Than are dreamt of in your philosophy.
—William Shakespeare, *Hamlet*

In 1978, thirty-one-year-old Stuart Cosgriff's future looked
bright. He worked for his father-in-law's business, a huge concern
called Mastercraft Fabrics, selling cotton and synthetic fabrics to
be draped across windows and stretched over furniture to make
homes more comfortable and sophisticated. Stu's business took
him all over New York State, and he often drove for long hours.
The trip he made in the late afternoon of March 17 that year
found him driving on the Long Island Expressway toward Manhattan, looking forward to the descent into the dark mouth of the
Queens–Midtown Tunnel. It was a familiar journey: Stu would
enter the underworld beneath the East River and then climb out
of the tunnel to see the light reflecting off the skyline of Manhattan. After traversing midtown Manhattan, he anticipated arriving
at his home in Tenafly, New Jersey, to his wife and children.

But as John Lennon sang, life is what happens to you while you're busy making other plans. Stu was driving along the section of the expressway approaching the tunnel when a few cars in front of him got tangled up in one of those spontaneous fender benders that seem to come out of nowhere but can snarl traffic for infuriating hours. Stu heard cars smacking into one another, brakes squealing, plastic bumpers crunching as they whacked into metal doors and fenders. Stu jammed on his brakes and was able to avoid the collision. He was fine, with not a scratch on him or his car, but he could see someone else who was not, a young woman struggling to open her banged-in door and get out of her car. Drivers were already beginning to exchange insurance information, and Stu could tell that the woman wanted to join in. Jumping into action, he was able to get her car door open; the woman, whose name was Margaret Poloskey, got out and thanked him.

Things had begun to return to normal. Heartbeats slowed, and the adrenaline rush dissipated. As Stu and Margaret began chatting calmly, though, they heard a screech of brakes that sounded as if a jet taking off from Kennedy Airport had overshot the runway and was about to land on the wide strip of the Long Island Expressway. But it wasn't a plane that was rocketing at them. A fully loaded eighteen-wheel tractor-trailer, without the capability to stop as quickly as a car one-twentieth its weight, was plowing into a dark blue van just behind Stu and Margaret. In the few seconds it took them to realize what was happening, the truck had careened into the rear of the van with such impact that it sent the smaller vehicle hurtling like a grisly billiard shot straight at the pedestrians standing on the five-lane highway.

The van ricocheted into Margaret. Then, in virtually the same moment, its bumper ripped into Stu's legs and tossed him in the air like a broken doll. He landed with a thud on the road. When Stu opened his eyes, he realized that he was on his back. He could see Margaret lying in a twisted heap not far away, and he knew she was dead. As his thoughts moved from sorrow for her to concern for himself, Stu spied something white and about the length of a finger with some red on its edges. In a sickening moment, he realized that he was looking at his own bone, lying next to his left leg. His trousers were slashed open, and he could see the bone of his left leg sticking out of his shin.

In the ensuing din of ambulance and police sirens, the flash of their lights, and the rush of emergency personnel, Stu wanted only to communicate one thing: "Call my father. He's a doctor."

As I was to learn, Stu's father was more than merely a doctor who prescribed treatments. Stuart W. Cosgriff, a clinical professor of medicine at Presbyterian Hospital in New York City from 1951 to 1983, had led teams into an important area of research in saving lives. He published well-respected and often cited reports on anticoagulant treatments and had been part of the medical team that had treated Bob Hope, among other public figures.

Upon hearing of the disaster that would make the centerfold of the *Daily News*, Dr. Cosgriff assembled a world-class medical team to address the challenges posed by his son's traumatic injuries. Stu had what the surgeons described as an open fracture of the left leg with substantial bone loss. Stu would need an antibiotic drip to fight the invasion of germs that could kill him. Every bit of road dirt had to be washed off the bone, and the surgeon needed to perform a skin graft from the hip so the gaping wound that exposed the tibia could be properly sealed.

The surgery was successful, and it appeared that his leg could be saved, although it would need constant attention. By Stu's account, the accident put him in the hospital for three years. As he later described the results of the accident, "My lower left leg was smashed. Most of the bone between my knee and my foot was thrown out of my leg and . . . had to be transplanted from my hips." In addition, he said, "I had a dropped foot, so I have a fused ankle. All my toes were fused, and my foot has shrunk to a size ten—and my right foot's a twelve!"

For years after the accident, Stu was in and out of surgery. An elite medical team continued its attempt to reconstruct Stu's mobility, with the net result that he limped and dragged his left foot as if it were his ball and chain. On a really good day, with the aid of a massive amount of painkillers, Stu could shuffle across a room to hug his wife or walk a few steps with his children. He did not surrender to the pain, though he kept a constant supply of painkillers handy for use when needed. He limped into meetings, sat across from prospective clients, and went about his business.

At first Stu believed that the modern medical approach of surgery and drugs would restore his ability to walk. But it proved to be a major challenge to restore the blood flow to a severely traumatized limb that resembled a shattered landscape of twisted sinew, shrinking muscles, and delicate bone. On the surface, Stu bore the extensive scars of repeated surgeries. A decade after the accident, he started to experience muscle degeneration in his left leg, until his calf muscle atrophied to the point that his lower leg looked like a straight line.

After two decades, Stu's physicians saw danger ahead. For all those years Stu had fought a losing war, the battleground having shifted from the towers of Presbyterian Hospital to the Hospital for Special Surgery. On an evaluating visit to an orthopedic surgeon who was all too familiar with his case, Stu received the bitterest of news. The discoloration of his lower leg indicated a dangerously low blood flow. The surgeon pointed out that the foot had more than shrunk; it was also constantly enduring stress fractures, which were hard to treat. Each stress fracture compounded the problem, and scarring and swelling further reduced the blood flow around the shaky architecture of bone.

The foot could eventually become infected and kill Stu. The physicians could prescribe only one option. Stu was told in the most correct medical terms that, to avoid further complications, a surgeon would need to sever the lower leg. Stu would require an artificial limb, although the surgeon noted that he might end up with more mobility. Some people can play golf with an artificial limb—something that Stu could not currently do.

Stu decided that he needed to embrace the news with courage. He explained his deteriorating condition and the surgeons' recommendation to his family. In an attempt to distract himself during the process of deciding to lose the limb, Stu scheduled an appointment to have his hair done at an exclusive salon. But once again, fate took an unexpected turn. "Make me look good," Stu said to his stylist, Sasha, trying to make light of things. "I'm going to get my leg cut off next week!"

Sasha could maintain her composure under the most difficult circumstances. Stu's declaration rattled her for a moment, but then she suggested there might be an alternative course. "Stu," she said, "before you go ahead with the surgery, I want you to call someone." She gave him my number. Sasha called and told me of her friend's situation, and after a couple of days I got a call from Stu. He figured it couldn't hurt, and might help, so he made an appointment to see me.

Marc Wishengrad and Christy Musumeci later interviewed Stu about the decision to go through with the amputation. "Why don't I just get an artificial limb?" Stu said. "Because I would be pain free. I had almost come to grips, or thought I had, but talking to myself about cutting my leg off is one thing and what it would do for me. Talking to a doctor and having him describe the procedure and what would happen was alarming."

On February 17, 2001, on Stu's visit to my office, he related his medical history. After hearing the seemingly endless litany of surgeries and recoveries, I told him that I could help him. For Stu, it seemed almost cathartic to discuss the decision he was grappling with. And then he pulled his left pant leg up to his knee, holding my gaze while waiting for the expression he expected to register in my eyes. But I was not discouraged. "Typically when I fly on an airplane for business," Stu went on, "I prop my leg up on the armrest in front of me, and, par for the course, a flight attendant appears and tells me to remove my leg. Then I pull my pant leg up, and they just look and say, 'Oh, I'm very sorry,' and push on without a further word."

But the sight of Stu's bare leg did not elicit that reaction from me. It's hard to explain, but at that moment I knew the direction of Stu's life would be altered. What came over me was such a powerful sense of certainty that I went far out on a limb. "They're not going to amputate your leg," I said. "In fact, you'll be playing golf soon."

Stu seemed suspicious at first. "But my father is—"

I cut him off. "I don't care what you have been told," I said. "I am telling you, your leg will not be cut off, and it will begin to heal as of this day. In fact, you will soon be golfing on it."

Stu asked me what the fee would be. "There is no fee," I said.

"What's the catch?"

"There is no catch."

All I wanted was for Stu to agree to open his mind and submit to receiving something, to allow himself to experience an intervention whose mechanism was not understood or known to exist within his father's philosophy. He looked at me, and I looked at him against the backdrop of the towers of Rockefeller Center outside my office window. Stu resigned himself to try, and with that he rolled up his pant leg again and lay on the table.

Once he was comfortable, I began the process, actually a combination of several practices. It was as if I were multitasking, simultaneously entering a meditative state, allowing my nonlocal mind (or consciousness) to extend beyond me to incorporate Stu's limb. Then I allowed myself to surrender to a connection to Source, that ineffable energy that is given a name in all major languages in the world and known to exist in all great spiritual traditions. As I focused on Stu's leg, I maintained a heightened state of consciousness that had become for me like riding a bike, an activity that required no conscious effort, simply a will to begin.

I began to see the damaged tissue resulting from the accident and the necessary invasive procedures to save his life. I then felt a sensation that exceeded what I had previously experienced when focusing my consciousness on injured knees or fractured arms. In this situation, the traumatized area was quite extensive, and the change, visible on the surface, was equally substantial. It appeared to me that the extent of the healing was in direct proportion to the extent of the injury. The reaction was not as Dr. Muss, the cardiologist, had described, "What was unusual was . . . to watch my knee transform. . . ." No, this was more profound, and I became excited by what I was witnessing. The result was not limited to the surface tissue but was happening throughout the traumatized limb. The skin was puckering, but the opaque, pearlescent surface was giving way, and blood circulation was breaking into the lower limb and migrating to the cold, opaque foot.

I did not say anything as I worked. I was simply in a state of complete gratitude, as this represented a personal best for me too. I lifted my eyes for a moment and saw that Stu had a contented look on his face, so I continued for the balance of the twenty minutes. But as I was to learn, Stu had also felt something profound. He later described the sudden vibration of warmth that had flowed through his lower leg at that moment. The sensation as he characterized it on tape was "similar to being massaged: a feeling of warmth, gentle pressure, and comfort."

When the experience was over, Stu stirred from his relaxed state and sat up. He looked down at his left leg and foot. There were no mechanical manipulative forces at work, I had not reached over or touched his leg, yet something extraordinary had happened. "I now have normal color!" Stu said. After a moment, he gently slid off the table and, feeling the floor under his feet, took a tentative step. The dragging of his left foot was greatly diminished.

"I was very skeptical the first time," Stu said. "Am I thinking it's better because I want it to be better?" He took another step and then another. As he did, the idea occurred to him that he might be able to do something he had not done since 1978—walk without pain, and without risk of breaking a bone in his foot. The possibility illuminated his face with a broad smile.

What occurred over the next few weeks astonished Stuart Cosgriff and everyone around him. In front of his father, Stu walked confidently across the carpeted floor, his left foot making a steady heel-to-toe movement. "Careful, careful," his father warned. Stu kept on striding, though, his left foot no longer a ball and chain but increasingly resembling a normal foot. Then in the mirror he noticed something that he had not seen in decades: the indications of growth and regeneration of a calf muscle.

"I'm now able to move my foot in ways that I never could. I now have normal color. I can change the plant [of my foot]. I can do things I couldn't do," Stu said later. "I now go for walks, I can jump, I can do just about anything I want. He gave me a chance to walk, with my father, with my family, and I'm deeply appreciative."

Six weeks after seeing me, Stu was able to take a stroll on the grass of the Westchester golf club to which he belonged, swing his club, and drive a dimpled white ball down the fairway, announcing to his golfing foursome, "I'm playing pain-free for the first time in twenty years!"

Being more of a humanist than a deep believer in God, Stu told me he attributed the change in his leg to the energy he had felt in my office. He had no other way to comprehend something that defied the laws of physics and whose function existed outside the paradigm of Western medicine.

As Rupert Sheldrake wrote, historians have long known that, at any given time in the narrative of science, "phenomena that do not fit into the prevailing model or paradigm are dismissed or ignored or explained away. They are anomalies. Yet to the embarrassment of the reigning theories, they persist. Sooner or later science has to expand to include them."

When I first worked with Stuart Cosgriff, in 2001, I was really just in the foothills, beginning to explore the benevolent potential of consciousness for healthcare. Seven years later Stu returned and consented to have his progress archived for my documentary. He recalled his initial experiences after the accident. "When I went to the doctors," he said, "it was strictly, 'Well, there's not much that can be done.' Their only alternative was amputation."

As someone whose father was an esteemed med school professor and whose mother had been a chief emergency room nurse for years, Stu had been raised to appreciate the vast achievements in conventional medicine. As he put it, "Those were the guys who I thought knew what all the options were."

At the close of his taped interview, Stu had this to say about the results of his experience: "When I'm invited to play golf at Pebble Beach, and somebody says, 'Do you want to come? Do we need a cart?' I always say, 'Yeah, we need a cart to hold the beer—not for me to be able to play.'"

Stu's ending remark was not prompted by any question, but seemed to spring from his spontaneous desire to express his joy and gratitude. As I watched his interview, I resonated with Stu's enthusiasm in testifying to his tangible physical improvements.

He stood before the cameras rising on his toes and then lowering again, his regenerated calf muscle contracting and lifting his substantial frame with ease. "I attribute the improvement in my foot to the therapy I got," he said. "I can walk a normal gait. I'm just getting stronger and stronger."

Stu's improvement provided an anomaly in medicine—an anomaly that could not be easily dismissed. It also inspired physicians to begin to be more receptive to the potential benefit of integrating consciousness-based interventions with surgery. I began to meet doctors who were willing to risk censure to explore the potential of new modalities. And I felt exhilaration and hope for the future of healthcare.

# Chapter 13

SOMETHING OLD, SOMETHING NEW

> Science can only be created by those who are thoroughly imbued with the aspiration towards truth and understanding. The source of this feeling, however, springs from the sphere of religion.
>
> —Albert Einstein

> What has been will be again,
> what has been done will be done again;
> there is nothing new under the sun.
> —*Ecclesiastes 1:9*

Since I first realized the capacity to tap into the transformative power that can manifest change in physical tissue, I have continued to demonstrate this discovery before medical doctors in an effort to further truth and understanding. These doctors have consistently expressed their gratitude for the opportunity to explore effective healing modalities that they had not been taught in medical school. Seeing patients daily with a wide array of health challenges, these physicians are quick to appreciate the potential benefits to their clientele.

What's even more impressive is that these open-minded physicians have gone on record to testify to the efficacy of these modalities, even though science has yet to develop machines sophisticated enough to measure the agent that is responsible for transforming limbs, restoring faces, and healing bones. The question that these doctors and I shared was not *if* it was happening but *how*. The situation reminded me of the Wright brothers, who spent hours observing seagulls hovering over the sand dunes off Kitty Hawk, dreamed of the immense benefit to society once they figured out the mystery, and then created a new mode of transportation.

However, despite the enthusiasm of my fellow researchers, as patient stories began to leak out, my life was altered significantly by questions from physicians, scientists, and journalists. As the demands grew and physicians began to discuss with me the breadth and depth of what can be healed, my personal need to understand continued to evolve. And with that, the big questions came to the forefront of my mind.

1. Why me?
2. How was it that I had the capacity to realize these healings?
3. Were there others in the past, or are there other people currently living, who learned to tap into a transformative force?
4. And what, if any, application did this capacity have for manifesting change and overcoming obstacles in other fields of endeavor, whether social, cultural, political, or spiritual?

Although I wholeheartedly agree with Albert Einstein's statement that "The most beautiful and profound emotion we can experience is the sensation of the mystical," I also know that having a mystical experience and realizing a capacity to heal with no apparent explanation can be daunting. I remembered speaking with my sister, Cassie, after she had given birth to her first child, John Ryan. "They give you a baby," she said with a hearty laugh, "but they don't give you an owner's manual with instructions!" I felt much the same way. Here I had apparently ignited a potential to manifest change at will and help people, but I was not cognizant of how I had achieved it, or the nature of the source from which this capacity stemmed.

I had access to top physicians from Harvard, New York University, and Georgetown medical schools, yet they were equally challenged to provide the answers. Perhaps the most helpful input I received from a doctor came from a colleague at the Global Health Institute. Dr. Patricia Muehsam was on the faculty of Mount Sinai Medical School and was passionately dedicated to preparing future medical students for the emerging role of consciousness in healthcare. One day Dr. Muehsam summarized the situation for me. "Consciousness is the most potent mediator of change in the world," she said. "But the practice of medicine is light-years behind the significant revolutions in scientific thinking that have transformed our understanding of nature and consciousness—most notably the revolution of modern physics in the early twentieth century. Nor has it paid attention to the consciousness research currently being conducted. Were modern medicine to fully understand and accommodate these constructs, it could then acknowledge the omnipotent power of thought or consciousness both to cause *dis*-ease and to manifest healing, and would lead to breakthroughs in how we understand and experience health."

As the years went by and I met other physicians, the tide seemed to me to be turning ever so slightly. Physicians were gradually realizing the folly of the old idea that humans are simply mechanistic beings, brains within physical bodies, as opposed to the new paradigm that humans have not only physical bodies but also nonlocal minds, which extend beyond the confines of the brain itself, as well as spirits that cannot be physically identified. According to the old paradigm, medical doctors primarily treat only the body; psychologists treat the mind; and clergy treat the soul and spiritual issues. The new paradigm advocates treating body, mind, and spirit as one interconnected whole.

As I collaborated with more and more medical professionals, I was encouraged to learn that there was indeed a growing movement to integrate new modalities into healthcare to provide better outcomes for patients. Further, I learned that doctors take a sacred oath not to withhold any therapy that can heal patients. This has long been the tradition, as Dr. James Gordon cited in his book *Manifesto for a New Medicine*: "Very few surgical procedures which are not, as drugs are, subject to FDA approval have ever been through large-scale clinical trials. This is true of many long-used conventional diagnostic techniques and drugs: a 1978 study by the U.S. Congress' Office of Technology Assessment indicated that approximately 85 percent of all therapies and procedures that were commonly used by physicians and in hospitals had never received any kind of rigorous evaluation."

Despite this tradition to embrace new therapies that defy scientific understanding, however, a large group of medical professionals still clings to a materialistic view of the world and seems adamant in not informing patients about modalities based on a spiritual component. This group asks absolute loyalty to their thinking with the threat of censure to any physicians who open their minds to other ideas. Einstein captured this phenomenon succinctly with these prophetic words, as valid today as when he wrote them, some seventy years ago: "Great spirits have always found violent opposition from mediocrities. The latter cannot understand it when a man does not thoughtlessly submit to hereditary prejudices but honestly and courageously uses his intelligence."

Dr. Larry Dossey has perfectly captured this obstacle of ignorance: "What I am saying is that the psyche has ways of manifesting far beyond anything known to materialistic science," he wrote. "You need to get a feel for what's at stake here. The reason that many of the dedicated materialistic scientists are so infuriated over the mere discussion of prayer and distant healing is that it really begins to call into question their world view. It calls into question the adequacy of materialistic science, upon which these people have staked their careers, self-identity and self-esteem."

Stu Cosgriff summed up this issue in the previous chapter when, faced with the prospect of having his leg amputated, he said that, "coming from a medical family, I thought these guys had all the answers." I had to agree with Stu that science was missing something. But where to look? I had met doctors from the best medical schools and had spoken with and read works by top psychiatrists and psychologists, but I had not investigated the role of spirit or the soul in answering the four questions at the beginning of the chapter. I had not even thought to explore the knowledge in the sacred texts of the world's religions at the risk of being perceived as foolish.

My unwillingness to look in that direction changed when I happened across a book that eloquently addressed this topic. In *God for the 21st Century,* a compilation edited by Russell Stannard, I read about what has come to be known in medical circles as "the forgotten factor." Dale Matthews points out that there are now more than three hundred studies conclusively demonstrating the medical value of religious commitment. So, given the inability of the scientists I had met to provide an explanation for my capability, I decided that I would open my mind and consult a member of the clergy for the "missing factor" that might shed some light.

I wanted to get the benefit of a belief system other than a "material view" to gain some understanding of why I was able to do what I was doing, and from what source I was drawing the capacity to facilitate healings. I hadn't attended formal religious services since I left elementary school. So it was with a bit of trepidation that I decided to seek out clerical advice now.

The closest house of worship to me was the Church of St. Vincent Ferrer on Lexington Avenue and Sixty-sixth Street, and I set out for the one-block stroll from my apartment. I climbed the stairs of the redbrick building and entered the rectory next door. I approached a receptionist sitting behind a partition similar to the setup in a doctor's office. I said that I would like to speak to a priest. The woman asked if I had an appointment. "No," I said. "It's something of a rather pressing nature, and I just need a few minutes to discuss a personal issue."

"Are you a member of the church?"

"No, I'm not," I said. "I live in the neighborhood, though."

"I'm sorry," she said, "but we can't accommodate your request." She then handed me a clipboard with some papers to fill out to join the church, and another form to set up a meeting with a priest. This was not the way I had expected it to go, so I importuned the woman a little further, but to no avail. "I'm sorry," she repeated, "but we just can't help you."

Maybe I'd had the wrong idea after all, I thought. I turned and handed her back her clipboard. Maybe the bad rap churches had been getting in the popular media was well deserved after all. As I was approaching the exit, the door swung open, and there standing before me was a man in a windbreaker over a light blue wool sweater with a clerical collar poking out. He was holding a small piece of luggage similar to a carry-on bag.

As I blocked his path, he smiled, and I asked simply if he was a priest. He acknowledged the obvious, but when I started to ask him for a few minutes of his time, he cut me off. "Oh," he said, "I'm not a member of this parish. I'm just visiting New York City and staying at the rectory."

I really needed his help, though, and I wasn't going to take that as an answer. "I understand you are not from this church," I said. "But you are a priest, right? And I need to speak to a priest."

He tried to walk around me, but I locked eyes with him. "In thirty years I have never asked a priest for advice," I said, "but I really have a problem that requires a spiritual solution. I just need a few minutes of your time—that's it, just a few minutes, I promise." In retrospect I realize I was being pushy, but I figured I might as well go all the way.

He looked at me and lingered for a few seconds. "Okay," he said. "Wait here."

I couldn't believe it. Perhaps he wasn't just another "hollow collar" after all. "Let me drop my bag, and I will be right with you." He slid open the door to a parlor overlooking Lexington Avenue and led me to a couch. "Please have a seat," he said while he sat in an armchair across from me. As I looked at his eyes I could see that his demeanor had totally shifted. Here was an absolute stranger looking at me with genuine concern and empathy. "How can I help you?" he asked.

"My life has been dramatically altered by something that happened to me," I said. "I can't understand what it was, and I'm hoping you can help me understand what's going on."

I related how I had restored the wood carvings from an old church.

"Oh, you have a gift for sculpting," he said, "for restoration."

I then backed up and told the story about seeing the disfigured children going into the hospital, and my fervent wish to be able to use my gift for sculpting to restore people, especially children.

"That's a nice dream," he said.

But then I described how a pearl of light had coalesced, forming a ball in the air in front of my eyes, and suddenly exploded, blinding me for a few minutes.

"Oh my," he said. "What did you do?"

I finished the whole story, including squeezing the sponge filled with holy water into the mouth of the carving.

"All right," he said. "Let me see if I've got this right. You were praying . . ."

"No," I said. "I wasn't praying."

"You were sitting in a meditative state, speaking to God, right?"

"Well, yes," I said. "I suppose."

"And then you asked God for the gift of healing."

"No," I said. "I didn't."

"You said, 'Wouldn't it be wonderful if I could use my gift to heal people's disfigured faces?'"

"Well, yeah," I said. "That's true."

"And then you experienced this epiphany," he said, "this light that you saw and that then came into you."

"Okay."

"Whereupon you made an act of faith," he said simply. "You went and got some holy water, and you squeezed it on the carving."

"I guess you could call it that," I said.

"That," he said at last, "is an old story, a common story, one that has been repeated many times throughout the millennia." Then, as if in an effort to help me understand more, he continued. "You held in your heart a fervent wish, and God heard you."

I sat there stunned. He didn't seem at all confused by my narrative but appeared to grasp the experience in a nutshell. Nor did he show any sign of skepticism or doubt. Instead, he offered to set up a meeting with the local bishop. I was grateful but said no, thanks. "I would rather not," I added. "I'm working my way through this. So, there's nothing to fear?"

"No, not at all," he concluded. "You should be happy. It's a blessing."

As you can imagine, this came to me as very good news. Perhaps sensing that I wasn't totally convinced, he recommended that I look through the sacred scriptures, where I would find other examples of what he meant. Then he was silent. I think I stood first, and then he rose too. I expressed my genuine gratitude to him for offering an impromptu consultation with me. I pumped his hand enthusiastically. "Thanks a lot," I said. "I really mean it—that was very helpful."

The priest just kept looking at me, smiling but not saying anything, nodding slowly. Not knowing the protocol, I asked what I owed him. He laughed. "No charge," he said. "It was nice speaking with you."

I wished him a nice visit to the Big Apple, he thanked me, and I walked out. Hitting the street, I felt that I had benefited greatly, so I stepped into the foyer of the church next door and dropped a few bills in the donation slot. As I walked home, the only way I can describe it is that I felt liberated. I had the answers to three of my four questions.

*Why me?* Because I held the desire in my heart while in a deep meditative state talking with the Creator.

*How?* As the priest put it, the wish I expressed to the Divine was answered.

*Was I unique?* He had said that this is a story that repeats itself throughout time.

The only question that remained concerned the potential applications of the gift.

*Can this connection to the transformative source overcome obstacles in other fields of endeavor?* He hadn't answered that one. As they say, three out of four ain't bad, so I was still feeling happy and relieved.

When I arrived home, I decided to follow the padre's suggestion and do some research. After my parents' divorce, my dad married a pleasant Scottish woman who had graduated from Marymount Manhattan College. Like many American colleges, Marymount had been founded on Christian roots, and I remembered that when Dad had retired to Hobe Sound, Florida, she had left a Bible in the apartment. So I dug it out, dusted it off, and started to page through it, looking for what the priest had told me about people receiving gifts from a divine source. As I flipped through, the book seemed to open on Paul's First Letter to the Corinthians. As I read, I could barely believe my eyes:

*Now to each one the manifestation of the Spirit is given for the common good. To one there is given through the Spirit the message of wisdom, to another the message of knowledge by means of the same Spirit, to another faith by the same Spirit, to another gifts of healing by that one Spirit, to another miraculous powers, to another prophecy, to another distinguishing between spirits, to another speaking in different kinds of tongues, and to still another the interpretation of tongues. All these are the work of one and the same Spirit, and he gives them to each one, just as he determines.*

I sat there stunned, meditating on what I'd just read. Here was the answer to my last question: "Now to each one the manifestation of the Spirit is given for the common good." In my twelve years of school and six years of college, I had never heard such ideas, that each person has a sacred inheritance, waiting to be claimed for the common good. From that day forward, I had a much better grasp of the picture—the science, the psychology, and the "missing factor."

Although I learned a great deal as a result of my consultation with the priest, it didn't inspire me to become religious in the conventional sense. As I have studied the works of some of the greatest doctors of medicine and divinity, I have come to realize that they share a common appreciation for the latent sacred potential that resides in each and every one of us. And whenever I experience connecting to Source and serving as a conduit for healing, I am reassured that this healing force is present everywhere in the universe. I have every confidence that in the future we will see people manifesting great changes for the good of humanity in all fields. The horse is out of the barn, and we need to redefine what it means to be human.

# Chapter 14

PLANTING SEEDS

> Imagine a gardener who has just planted an extraordinary and unique seed in the earth. If he is so stupid and vain that he wants everyone to know it, and he digs up the seed to show every visitor, saying: "Do you see this? I planted it; take a good look, because it will become an exceptional tree with delicious fruits, and soon we will be eating them. . . ." You must not remove the seed from the earth; wait until, on its own, the tree becomes visible to others.
>
> —O. M. Aïvanhov

Manifesting the life you were created to live is in my mind the highest and most rewarding use of your life. Marching to your own inner heartbeat into the Promised Land, however, is not a simple matter. It is a journey that will require making a strong decision, connecting to a higher power, and taking bold action.

Only then will the time arrive that you, your family, and your larger family of humanity will have the opportunity to enjoy the banquet you are planning for them.

But then nothing worth accomplishing comes into being without persistence. As William James said, "A new idea is first condemned as ridiculous and then dismissed as trivial, until finally it becomes what everybody knows." We know from the great manifesters, who all followed the five steps that I am about to list (and that I will describe in much greater detail in Part II), that, when climbing the mountain, the first steps, the foothills, are relatively easy. But then the incline steepens before your inner eye can see the shape of your dream coming into focus on the horizon.

In my particular journey,

1. I looked at the world around me. I looked within myself and unearthed the suppressed desire to help broken people be restored.

2. I decided to do something about it. I didn't know how, but I made a covenant with myself that I would be part of the solution, that I would join the kindred spirits rising all over the planet to transform the face of healthcare.

3. Then I connected to a profound transformative source that is known by many names—the Field, the Beloved, the Divine—but that I call God.

4. For years I had been acting, but although I was sticking with my plan and keeping my eyes on the prize, I had not received any recognition from the public, the healthcare system, or my family. And I had yet to reap any financial reward for the seeds of my research.

5. Now I was on the last steps up the mountain, but I had yet to manifest my larger dream. And, as William James had so clearly defined the last stage in the manifestation of a new

idea, I wanted the people in the healthcare system to open their minds and hearts to embrace it until it became "what everybody knows." I wanted everyone to know that what all religions had promised, and what quantum physics is now saying is theoretically possible, is actually true: We all possess a sacred potential that if ignited will empower us to literally transform human tissue to such an extent that it will be obvious to all.

I had learned many lessons from many people of all backgrounds and all belief systems. An Asian sage had once said to his students, "For every discipline that you learn there are multiple applications." I had learned certain military lessons earlier in my life that twenty years later I could apply to advancing the evolution of the healing arts. Knowledge and discovery can be used for healing or hurting depending on the level of the consciousness of the person or institution wielding the discovery.

While a cadet midshipman in the U.S. Maritime Administration, I had the privilege of having lunch with Admiral Sheldon H. Kinney, the president of the university, in the officers' dining room. Admiral Kinney was a graduate of the U.S. Naval Academy and of the National War College and had served after his retirement from the armed forces as professor of law and policy science at the State University of New York Fort Schuyler. While discussing the colossal task of preparing the university's training ship to embark on its journey, Admiral Kinney told me that the work required many skills: overhauling the engines, calibrating the radars, stocking stores for a month at sea, and painting the ship from stem to stern. "A leader does not need to possess the knowledge to execute each task," he pointed out, "but a great leader needs to know how to recognize talent and delegate responsibilities to able people."

This little pearl of wisdom has influenced my entire life since that day. I thought about this lesson as I was pondering how to embark on the last leg of my journey to manifest the integration of consciousness-based healthcare. As I planned how to manifest this change, I remembered a lesson I had learned from studying another great leader—not a leader of warriors but a fighter for peace, Mahatma Gandhi: "A small body of determined spirits fired by an unquenchable faith in their mission can alter the course of history."

So, integrating the wisdom of the lessons from the graduate of the war college Admiral Kinney with the words of the peacekeeper Gandhi, I took the best from both master strategists and began to formulate a strategy.

1. Recognize talent.
2. Delegate responsibilities to able people.
3. Assemble a small body of determined spirits fired by an unquenchable faith in their mission.

## Assembling a Team

After my discovery in 2000 of the capacity to transform human tissue, I began to encounter a number of able-bodied professionals, each of whom shared two important characteristics: an unquenchable faith in the mission to evolve healthcare and a desire to integrate newly discovered modalities that were demonstrating benefit but that conventional medicine was slow to embrace. So we set about assembling a team of cross-disciplinary professionals including Dr. Patricia Muehsam, on the faculty of Mount Sinai Medical School; Dr. Peter Roche de Coppens, professor of sociology, anthropology, and psychotherapy at East Stroudsburg

University in Pennsylvania and the Sorbonne in Paris; Dr. Beverly Rubik, a biophysicist who had conducted scientific research in mind-body, subtle energies, and complementary medicine; Dr. J. Mackenzie Stewart, who served on the board of the Texas Association of Acupuncture and Oriental Medicine and on the faculty of Southwest Acupuncture College; and Dr. John E. Mack, professor at Harvard Medical School and Pulitzer Prize–winning biographer. During that process, I also encountered Alex Donner, who was on the board of the William Donner Foundation. Alex was a New York–based attorney from a very old New England family, and with his endorsement we received a small grant of seed money.

In 2003 we drafted a mission statement for what would become the Global Health Institute, a not-for-profit educational and research foundation. With the guidance of the medical doctors and scientists at the institute, assisted by a few dedicated lay members with skills in law and nonprofit administration, and with the generous pro bono work of an attorney, we began to make serious plans to move to the next level.

The team I was working with was engaged in the discovery, replication, and archiving of the effects of a new modality to support the efficacy of consciousness-based healthcare. What we discovered and archived would create a body of evidence for a wonderful secret that only a few doctors had witnessed and testified to, and a handful of participants and laypeople knew about.

## A Great Debate Ensues

We subsequently hired professional consultants with success in launching conservative medical products and services. They joined us in meeting with medical doctors, doctors of philosophy, lawyers, and theologians united by the intention to determine the course the foundation needed to take to achieve it goals. Peter Roche de Coppens offered a quotation from Albert Einstein that was quite familiar to the doctors and philosophers in the room: "Significant problems we face cannot be solved at the same level of thinking we were at when we created them."

We all began to debate how we would roll out our work. Would we first educate physicians, students, and the public, and have the audacity to challenge the currently ordained wisdom of a materialist belief system? Some of the medical doctors suggested, for instance, that we take our body of evidence to peer-reviewed medical journals and request that they publish it. But as some of the scientists on the board pointed out, most medical journals won't publish evidence of modalities until they can discover the "mechanism" that explains scientifically what action is causing a given reaction. This policy, however, raised the daunting challenge of approaching the conservative bodies that finance such research and asking them to underwrite something beyond their comprehension. This is illustrated by the words of legendary Irish boat builders: "'Tis a difficult ordeal to approach the patrons who hold the purse, to finance a journey to set sail on a voyage about the globe, when the patrons who hold the purse believe the world to be flat."

And then there was the moral question, Should we wait to announce a therapy that could save limbs and lives every day, and permit people to suffer needlessly while we go about establishing our case? Armand Fried, a New York attorney who had earned a reputation as a hard-nosed litigator, had had a change of heart when he was permitted to observe the work on a family member. "There is a moral imperative to teach," Armand insisted. "If you can save lives or save limbs, then really we must teach." And there was ample precedent in medical tradition. Dr. James Gordon had pointed out that the majority of therapies and procedures, including surgeries, used in hospitals have never undergone rigorous studies. They are used daily around the world for one simple reason: they work.

## The Decision

We decided that we would go public with the body of evidence and seek professionals to assist us: from Emmy-nominated filmmakers with expertise in filming medical procedures to talented writers and experts in introducing new ideas. We would simultaneously welcome scientists to participate in research over the coming years. The chair of the Medical Advisory Board engaged a Harvard-trained research scientist to prepare a project overview.

Today, many of the seeds planted then are beginning to bear fruit. Through collaborative efforts with doctors from leading medical schools, academic institutions, and other nonprofit organizations across the country, the Global Health Institute is educating health professionals, students, and the media on the discoveries, cutting-edge therapies, and emerging knowledge that is shaping the new model of healthcare. The foundation also collaborates with and participates in research projects that generate empirical evidence demonstrating the viability and efficacy of integrating medicine for the benefit of all patients. Finally, the institute archives its explorations for researchers and students. We make available information on our endeavors through a website, lectures and presentations, and short educational films.

In my current role as director of consciousness studies, I pioneer research about the potential of consciousness to be a mediator of healing. Working with a team of medical doctors, research scientists, biophysicists, and theologians, I continue to explore how the application of consciousness results in tangible benefits in the body of the subject. To quote Dr. John Mack, "We aren't trying to determine *if* it works. We're beyond that. We are trying to understand *how* this works."

I want to emphasize that the Global Health Institute is not a healthcare provider. The cutting-edge work described in this book is not yet available at clinics or hospitals, or to the general public directly from me. Participants for ongoing studies are typically recruited through advertising aimed at medical schools or the general population. The Global Health Institute has maintained its administrative office in New York City since 2004 and conducts its studies at clinical facilities around the country. To learn more about projects and presentations we sponsor, please visit our website, www.ghifoundation.org.

We are currently seeking to embark on studies exploring non-invasive interventions that hold the potential to treat a wide variety of conditions which are currently untreatable or for which current treatment protocols can be improved. Examples include studies designed to

- gauge the effectiveness of consciousness-based healthcare in accelerating postsurgical rehabilitation, with the potential to significantly reduce the length of hospital stays
- accelerate the reduction in swelling following head trauma to preclude the onset of coma, or to treat those who have already succumbed to comas. (This could prevent the necessity of drilling holes in the skull to relieve pressure—still an everyday practice in this country)
- reduce scoliosis in adolescent women before implementing more invasive surgical methods, such as attaching a steel bar (called a Harrington rod) to the spine
- regenerate muscle mass after prolonged convalescence.

Preliminary case studies in these treatment areas have demonstrated significant enough promise to warrant the full clinical studies that would be needed to make these treatments available in hospitals worldwide.

That's clearly an ambitious program, and we realize that the institute needs to present incontrovertible proof of what we are saying—that through intention the mind can direct consciousness to migrate into a person and physically transform tissue. And so, following our formative discussions and debates, the Global Health Institute decided that it was time to select the case that would best demonstrate the potential this discovery holds. We chose a case that had taken place several years earlier but that we could document through before-and-after photographs and a filmed interview with the subject. This would present evidence that could not be dismissed—evidence that was as plain as the nose on your face.

# Chapter 15

## MANIFESTING MICHELANGELO

Beauteous art, which, brought with us
from heaven, will conquer nature; so
divine a power.

—Michelangelo

During the early days of my work, as I walked to my office I could see on my left a great monument to a higher power, the spires of St. Patrick's Cathedral ascending 330 feet into the sky as an enduring symbol of New York's spiritual history. Yet just across Fifth Avenue, on my right, pure reason in the form of the seventy-story, steel-and-granite tower known worldwide as 30 Rock, the crowning glory of the Rockefeller empire, dwarfed the cathedral, casting a shadow on that white-marble-and-stained-glass testament to belief in the Divine. Inside Rockefeller Center's lobby, a large mural glorifying "Man's Intellectual Mastery of the Material Universe" portrayed the technological advances of the human race financed by the prophets of commerce, and in the plaza the bronze statue of Atlas balanced the globe as if about to hurl the achievements of man's material accomplishments into the face of the Creator. The cathedral had once been the tallest building in New York City, but the towers of the new prophets have long since come to dominate the city's skyline.

In that first office that I rented from a mapmaker, I thought of the challenges I would have to overcome to shift the zealous believers in the material paradigm that still ruled the roost into the twenty-first century. However, change was in the air, and, as the Virgin Airways founder and maverick entrepreneur Richard Branson said, "It is the bloated massive industries that are in most ripe need of transformation." Perhaps I didn't possess the assets of this champion of change, but like every other individual who had ushered in a transformation to benefit humanity, I did possess an enthusiasm and commitment to be part of the solution. I wanted to map out the path that I discovered, the process that others could follow to ignite the power of their consciousness to manifest change.

I realized that I faced a formidable task: How was I to effect a change in thinking about something the current generation's "experts" considered impossible? For many months now, I had been healing children, medical doctors, children of medical doctors, laypeople, and clergy, much to their amazement. They would express their gratitude and shock while limbs were transformed and skin "puckered." I had already begun to document some of the more interesting case histories, as I have described in Chapter 11. But I realized that I needed the kind of visibly arresting evidence that would be plain for anyone to see. In short, I needed to document a case suitable for the media.

I sat in the quiet and pondered the obstacles. I needed an encounter with someone whose condition was beyond the current capacity of medicine, someone whose face was so severely disfigured that his or her illness was outside the ability of man or machine to correct. It would have to be a condition that could be resolved only by connecting to the transformative force of a higher power, so that the results would be plain for all to see. I couldn't know then that the answer to my prayers lived not far away from me, in the Bronx. His name was Sammy, and, like me, he was in need of a miracle.

Sammy was born in 1977 with a problem that would create crisis after crisis throughout his childhood. Sammy's youth was not filled with long hours spent on the playground with his pals or enjoying the normal stages of growth. Instead, from birth his years were marked with regular visits to hospitals and operating tables. Most children open their eyes to see the beautiful face of a loving mother looking down at them. Sammy quite often saw men and women in white and blue surgical masks staring down at him with deep concern. By Sammy's count, he had had at least thirty operations before he was twenty. His mother stopped counting after the fiftieth time Sammy inhaled anesthesia and his face awaited the surgeons' scalpels and saws.

What caused his appearance to be so different from that of other children? Doctors don't believe that Sammy's condition was inherited, genetic, or the result of environmental toxins. He suffered from a condition called amniotic band syndrome (ABS, also known as temporal band syndrome). A set of congenital birth defects, ABS takes many forms, but the disfigurements are probably caused when the face, a limb, fingers, or toes are trapped by stringlike amniotic bands in the womb. Babies develop in the uterus surrounded by a protective sac, the amnion, which during pregnancy is filled with amniotic fluid. No doctor can say with certainty why the womb, designed to protect a baby while it grows, can sometimes break down and become an unwitting enemy.

In Sammy's case, fibers of the amnion separated and drifted toward him, as if spun out by some sea spider. The fibers wrapped around Sammy's right hand as he grew, and the hand became

webbed, as if he were destined to be an amphibian. Most threaten-
ingly, the bands wrapped around the unborn baby's face, molding
a huge cleft palate, stunting the development of his cheekbones,
and damaging the cornea of one of his eyes. The cleft palate
made it difficult for Sammy to be nourished. He cried when he
was born, his mouth veering sharply up in an inverted V. Even in
those rare moments when he attempted to smile, Sammy's face
resembled the contorted figure in Edvard Munch's famous painting, *The Scream*.

When Sammy was born, baby photos were taken, as is customary, but unlike other mothers, Anna will never show anyone
a picture of Sammy's infant face. She once took Sammy to the
doctor's office through the front door. A woman saw the bundle
in Anna's arms and offered the customary "What a lovely child."
As Anna tells the story, when the woman saw Sammy's face, with
that gash of a cleft palate, she qualified the compliment with "Oh,
my God, he's a monster!" After that anguishing experience, Anna
took her child in through the back door of the clinic. It was as if
Sammy's deformity had been dreamed up by a demon.

The problem for Anna—and for Sammy—was that the world is
not filled with back doors, with private entrances where you can
escape the stares and taunts of children and insensitive adults. On
occasion Anna had to walk on the mean streets of the Bronx and
listen to people taunting Sammy. Making matters even worse,
Sammy's father had abandoned them.

At the age of seven months, Sammy received a cornea trans-
plant, but his left eye could not be saved, and Sammy's schooling
was affected. He tried to learn his lessons with just one eye, but
that one was surrounded by puffiness that handicapped his vision.
To Sammy the world seemed like a cruel blur.

Like any mother in her position, Anna hoped for a miracle, but
the course of Sammy's childhood offered little hope. The doctors

were heroic. Yet as they worked to right his physical wrongs, they also inflicted massive pain. Powerful opioids blunted some of the pain caused by the invasive procedures. Sammy's doctors needed to remove his nose so they could improve his facial bone structure. Sammy's shapeless, swollen nose was detached, lifted from his face, and placed in a special icebox. At the end of the procedure, surgeons reattached the nose and made sure that Sammy had the necessary painkillers.

All the noble efforts of the doctors had bought Sammy relatively little respite from his suffering. True, they had changed a face that in the nineteenth century would have destined Sammy to appear in a carnival show, where people so afflicted could at least earn a living and survive by the coins they could attract from a public whose reactions swung from pity to revulsion. Still, the end result was to make Sammy appear as if he had been beaten with a baseball bat. Anna was never bitter, and Sammy struggled daily with the desire to live and the question of why God would do this to him.

At one point Sammy was introduced to Cher, the singer and movie star who appeared in the film *Mask,* about a child with a similarly disfiguring condition. Cher had been raising money for the Children's Craniofacial Association, and through her Sammy received support and encouragement from the association. He even appeared on *The Maury Povich Show* in an effort to raise awareness, but that did little to alleviate the emotional pain of living with a face from which most people involuntarily recoiled.

Sammy's life sometimes overwhelmed him, and the ache he felt in his heart for love as reflected in the lyrics of one of his favorite bands, seemed destined to worsen: "I just need someone to love." If only someone would answer Sammy's cry of the heart! When he was very young, Sammy wrote a poem that gives a sense of what he was feeling.

Random thoughts here and there
Random thoughts but no one cares
I feel so hurt and lonely inside
To the point that I want to die
You ask me why and I try to explain
But no one truly feels my pain
It hurts so much it makes me cry
I don't understand, why, oh, why

Sammy was brought to my attention by a professor of photography at Harvard who was a pioneer in facial recognition software technology and a staunch advocate for children. Nancy had volunteered her professional photography skills to document the challenges of children who suffered from various kinds of craniofacial deformities and focus attention on their plight. I was unaware of Nancy's work, yet she had heard about mine. She thought I might be able to apply my own pioneering work to assist one of the kids she was trying to help. When she first met Sammy, her heart went out to this sweet kid. She wanted to change his world for the better. As Nancy spoke about Sammy, I grew more and more excited. I told her that I would love to meet Sammy and his mother.

Nancy arranged for us to meet at her photography studio, and when I arrived she cautioned me. "What you're about to see," she said, "may be a little disturbing. Sammy is severely disfigured."

"I've seen people maimed at sea," I said. "I've looked into the thoracic cavity while observing open heart surgery. I think I can handle it."

Still, when I saw Sammy for the first time, I had to control my reaction. I'd never seen a face so badly distorted, and my heart went out to him. I walked over to where Sammy was sitting, and I looked at him, although his face was turned to the side. He wouldn't look at me, so I gently took hold of his pinkie and gave it a little tug. "Sammy," I said, but he still wouldn't look at me. I said his name again, and he finally looked up into my eyes. What I saw reminded me a little of the day I looked at the big clump of clay that I had put on the nose of that old wooden church carving in my workshop. I felt as Michelangelo might have when he described the elation in finding the rough block of Carrara marble he had been searching for to sculpt a masterpiece. "I saw the angel in the marble," Michelangelo said, "and carved to set him free." In the same way, I wanted to set the inherent beauty in Sammy's face free from its rough form. The tissue around his eyes was puffy, and a scar ran down the center of his forehead. Another scar ran from the corner of Sammy's left eye across to his ear. And in the middle of his face was a mass that resembled a shapeless lump of mashed potatoes.

I looked him in the eye. "Sammy," I said, "I believe you can be helped. We're going to release a beautiful nose from your face."

Then he looked at me. "For real?" he asked.

"Yeah," I said. "You're going to have a beautiful nose." I was smiling, and he could see that it wasn't a polite, forced smile. I couldn't help feeling that Sammy's tragedy was the answer to my prayer. Then I felt a pull on my shirtsleeve. It was Nancy.

"I've got to talk to you," she said. Sammy's mother was looking on, so Nancy pulled me into the hall. "You really can't tell him that," she said, "because you're giving him hope. And the hope . . . if it doesn't happen, it's going to hurt him deeply. He's been under the knife so many times that his hope's about gone, you know? He writes songs about suicide. He sits at home thinking that his dream of an acting career will never come true, and that no one besides his mother will ever love him. He'll never have friends, he'll never have anything."

"Nancy," I said, "it's going to happen." She finally relented but then explained that there was another challenge: Anna could not afford to pay me. I assured Nancy that there was no fee for my work on children.

When Sammy's mother brought him to my office later that week, he came in looking at his feet, with the hood from his stretched sweatshirt covering his head and part of his face, giving him the appearance of a reclusive monk. Nancy took some "before" photos for the record. She reminded me that the torturous process by which Sammy's malformed nose had been removed and later reattached had been repeated many times. Now his nose was just a mound of gray tissue devoid of blood flow. The abundance of scarring and the absence of blood flow precluded further surgery on that part of his face.

As Sammy lay on my table, Nancy was looking over my shoulder. I closed my eyes, visualizing Sammy as if he had never suffered, as if all the scars and indignities of his life had already faded from him. I imagined Sammy with an attractive nose. Creating a vision in my mind's eye, I held the image like a holograph over the mass in the center of his face. Next, I made a conscious effort to purge any remaining vestiges of doubt from my mind. I had an audience and was a bit anxious, as might be expected. This was new territory for me, the most challenging work I had faced so far.

Sammy asked if it was going to hurt. I smiled, because his question distracted me from my anxiety. I had good news for Sammy. "No, you're going to be fine," I said. "You won't feel any pain. Actually, you're going to enjoy it!" I focused all of my intention on the rough, swollen lump of gray flesh masquerading as a nose.

It grew very silent, as if the people in the room were holding their breath beneath the bright lights set up for the photography. I told Sammy to close his eyes. When I could see he was comfortable, I closed my own eyes, and a smile grew on my face, as a feeling of gratitude for this opportunity entered my mind. I took a moment to feel the gratitude for the universe conspiring so perfectly to bring Sammy and Nancy together, and then to permit this meeting to happen. I allowed my thoughts to go silent and my body still. I sat erect on the stool, my feet on the foot rail, and relaxed as I permitted my consciousness to expand beyond the confines of my body. I allowed it to grow until I became one with the transformative force that is everywhere, beneath every rock and within all things, as it says in the ancient Gnostic scriptures I had read: "Split a piece of wood and I am there. Lift up the stone, and you will find me there."

This ability to connect to the all-pervasive, transformative force, the Field, the divine spirit, was now part of my life like the act of walking. It took me only a minute each morning to maintain this uniquely human capacity to connect to the Source of all life, just a bit longer than it took my computer's wireless antenna to access the unseen signal that permeates the city where I live. As my eyes remained closed, the feeling of connection to the Divine became palpable. I opened my eyes and, maintaining the connection like an Eastern yogi meditating, a priest deep in the contemplative practice of walking a labyrinth, a rabbi praying, a Sufi dervish spinning, an American Indian entering the circle of the Sun Dance, an inspired artist channeling a masterpiece, I too was connected.

I allowed my gaze to rest on Sammy's face. I loaded the intention that I had set moments before into my mind, the way a painter visualizes his painting before he touches the canvas or a golfer sees her shot before she swings. I allowed an empathetic connection to form in my heart, linking the two of us in a way unseen but as real as the love of a parent for a child. And then I prepared to begin, as if I were the pilot of a jetliner sitting on the tarmac with the engines whirring, ready for takeoff at the signal from the tower. I shifted my focus from the wonderful sensation of my body humming to the vibration of creation and willed my consciousness to expand from me to migrate across the three feet that separated me from Sammy and permeate the skin on his face. Consciousness imbued with intention rippled outward and gently touched Sammy's face, permeating the tissue as if it were not solid at all but a dense mass of vibrating molecules.

At that instant, something began to happen. The scars that marked where Sammy's nose had been reattached to his cheeks began to break down, to shrink, as if they were lumps of lead melted away by some unseen torch. I turned to look over my shoulder at Nancy, who was photographing the process. "Are you seeing what I'm seeing?" I asked.

Nancy's camera clicked away. She pulled the camera momentarily away from her cheek and smiled, a faint mist welling in her eyes. "Yes," she said. "I am."

Anna's eyes were also full of tears. We all watched as Sammy's nose was transformed. The rough mass of tissue began to melt more quickly, like snow receding in the summer off a mountaintop, releasing the shape of an attractive nose.

We took a short break. As Nancy took a few more pictures, I recalled the visit of a woman the previous day who had left a CD by her favorite artist, Mahalia Jackson, the great gospel singer whose music had inspired so many in the civil rights movement. So I put the disk in my CD player, and out came the inspired voice of that gifted singer: "We shall overcome." I had goose bumps all over my body from the music and said to Nancy, "Are you ready?"

Sammy was out like a log on a sunny beach under the lights. Nancy picked up her professional Nikon. "Yes," she said, "I'm ready."

"Okay," I said, connecting to the Source and willing the transformation to continue. Instantly the process of change began again, exactly as Dr. Muss had described when I worked on her damaged knee. The skin started to pucker, and the shape transformed before our eyes. The process slowed and the previously lifeless, gray, dappled skin gave way to the warm, pink skin of a healthy child's face.

The photos Nancy took that day memorialized something transcendent that matched her published account of what she witnessed. Sammy's misshapen nose was reduced in size by one-third. The swelling around his eyes was also reduced, improving Sammy's vision. When we were done, Sammy went into the bathroom, where there was a mirror. Mirrors had never been kind to him, but now he looked and saw the emergence of a normal face. As he pulled on his hooded sweatshirt to leave my office, I asked him what his plans were for the day.

He said he'd probably go home and watch television. I was in such a state of gratitude for his having come into my life that I handed him a few folded bills and patted his shoulder. "Go to the movies," I said, "and have some fun."

When Sammy exited the building, onto the crowded street, he hadn't slipped his hood over his face. He was not staring at his feet in shame, and he no longer carried himself like a person trying to avoid the constant stares of passersby. Sammy strolled up Fifth Avenue past St. Patrick's Cathedral, Rockefeller Center, Cartier, and Tiffany, and the same sun that made the diamonds sparkle in the windows of those fine shops touched his face. When the river of Christmas shoppers and sightseers exiting Rockefeller Center with their shopping bags and ice skates passed him, none of the adults looked at Sammy, none of them seemed to notice Sammy at all, and the children ignored him too. For Sammy, that felt like a miracle come true.

When Sammy walked out of my office, I felt profound humility and gratitude. Indeed, I was probably more grateful to Sammy than he could know. Because of his life intersecting with mine, my childhood dream of a career in healthcare, my lifelong desire to help people, had been made manifest for me. I would never look back and wish for another path. I had discovered my purpose for being. At last I could see that some divine plan had shaped my existence, and all the events that had caused me pain along the way began to make sense. And for Sammy, the dream of having a career as an actor, which he had been told to abandon, as a child, was now a possibility.

When I left my office that day, I had butterflies in my stomach. I had not yet seen Nancy's photographs, but I felt a certainty, a kind of knowing, the same knowing I'd had as a nine-year-old boy in Beach Lake when Jim spun that Wheel of Chance. But I wasn't playing for childhood toys anymore. I was an adult now; I had put away those childish ways and wanted to manifest a tangible benefit for humanity. I had a sensation that in the near future the world would have to accept the shattering of old limits and the emerging of new truths. We as a species would have to embrace an expanded view of our own potential, and redefine what it means to be human.

# PART II

## THE FIVE STEPS

# Chapter 16

HOW TO MANIFEST THE CHANGE
YOU WANT TO SEE IN THE WORLD

I have a dream.
—Martin Luther King, Jr.

Be the change you want to see in the
world.
—Mohandas Gandhi

Others have seen what is and asked
why. I have seen what could be and
asked why not.
—Robert F. Kennedy

Plenty of people would have you believe that you are small and
insignificant, that some problems are so insurmountable no one
individual can do anything to change them, no matter how much
you may want to. This is not true. You, the reader, possess a sacred

potential to manifest the change you want to see in the world. Along with the three luminaries whose words open this chapter, the person I believe has best captured this concept of unlimited potential is Marianne Williamson. Her words in her book *A Return to Love* express the underlying belief that I want to communicate here. "Your playing small does not serve the world."

As I said in my invitation at the beginning of this book, I believe that we all possess a purpose and the sacred potential to achieve it. We are all born with gifts, qualities, and personal convictions that make us unique. Just as your fingerprints belong to nobody else in precisely the pattern they form on your hands, so are your feelings, emotions, and convictions particular to you. Each of us is uniquely qualified to manifest change in the world. As the sacred collection of sayings discovered by a farmer in the desert put it so perfectly, "If you bring forth what is within you, what you have will save you."

When I was at a low point in my life, despairing that I would ever find the path I was meant to follow, my friend Mitchell Nochlin lifted me up by telling me not to worry because I was "uniquely qualified for a job yet to be created." Behind his sense of humor was great compassion and genuine insight. I realized that I had to stop trying to fit my round peg into the square holes being offered as my only options. All I needed was a ray of hope that my purpose was hiding just beneath the surface, waiting for me to uncover it.

The world is full of opportunities for improvement and for using your sacred gift. In whatever field of endeavor you may be involved, you will find a cornucopia of challenges waiting to be resolved. For each lock there is a key, and for each problem there is a person uniquely qualified to unlock the solution. Each challenge is waiting for the one person to come along whose destiny it is to heal that issue. Not everyone who looks around and sets out to change the situation becomes as famous as Dr. King or Mahatma Gandhi. When I lived on Long Island, it seemed like almost everyone drove around drunk during the holidays and in the summer. Teenagers and adults alike would spend the night drinking beer on the beach or hanging out at bars and not give a second thought to driving home under the influence. That has changed drastically in recent years, mainly through the efforts of a couple of women who would be considered ordinary by most standards.

In 1980, Cari Lightner was killed by a repeat drunk-driving offender as she walked down a suburban California street. In response, her mother, Candy Lightner, founded Mothers Against Drunk Driving (MADD). Cindy Lamb—whose daughter, Laura, was the nation's youngest person to become a quadriplegic after their truck was hit at high speed by another repeat drunk driver— joined Lightner in her crusade. People continually told Lamb that "you can't change City Hall," but she took that as a challenge. Lightner and Lamb said the greatest problem they faced was the social acceptance of drunk driving as "just the way things are." Yet together these two women sparked a movement that has helped save hundreds of thousands of lives. Like them, many individuals hold dreams in their hearts, get their righteousness on, take a step in faith, and manifest the change they want to see in the world. And the rest is our future.

As all the great spiritual traditions have long promised, and the science of quantum physics is beginning to embrace, we possess an inherent capacity—not fully understood at this moment in time—to transform the environment around us. We can cocreate the world within which we live, whether that means changing laws, shattering social preconceptions, or inventing something that simply didn't exist before someone believed it was possible. The initiators of change—whether they are the first to run a four-minute mile or the first member of any minority to achieve a position of influence or power—merely enjoy the privilege of being first. Thereafter they have the pleasure of watching those who follow replicate what they have done and achieve even more. I am inviting you to ignite the sacred potential you have to manifest the change that is in your hearts.

The Five Steps that I'll be describing in this part of the book were present in many of my earliest recollections, but my conscious awareness of them developed gradually. Like most of the insights that led to my writing this book, the steps were not the results of an intellectual process. They evolved over the course of events and observations that occurred from childhood until very recently. They are embedded in the stories and parables that make up the first part of this book, because those events laid the groundwork for my understanding of the Five Steps. Now I will spell them out so that you can learn how to apply them in your own life.

As I said in my invitation at the beginning of the book, we are all born with a sacred potential to manifest change. I spent most of my early years ignorant of this potential and discovered how to manifest change only by stumbling upon the process. My whole life I had cast a wide net trying to find my purpose, and in a way the far-ranging elements of that search all worked together to guide me. The need to identify my purpose in life came home to me that day when I was sitting in Peter's Barber Shop waiting for a haircut and I happened to read the story about timeless wisdom hidden in the earth for nearly two thousand years. But that need had been planted much earlier, when as a teenager I observed my father after coming home from work, walking around our backyard, seemingly despondent, with a drink in his hand. When I asked my mother what was up, she revealed that, while they were still engaged, my father had been offered a Hollywood studio contract. But his prospective father-in-law had discouraged him from risking the steady income of a government job to follow his bliss and pursue a career in the movies. My mother's father had lived through the Great Depression and didn't want his daughter marrying someone who might be out of a job if things didn't work out in Hollywood. My father decided to abandon his dream and apparently regretted it the rest of his life.

Because he didn't bring forth what was within him, what he hadn't brought forth was eroding his spirit. Even as a child of ten, I made a promise to myself that I wouldn't let that happen to me. My friend Mitch Nochlin liked to repeat Gandhi's famous saying, "Be the change you want to see in the world." To become that change, I reconnected with my childhood dream to restore lives and health. I got out of my rational thinking mind and allowed my child's imagination free rein to dream of healing. That was the moment that ignited my sacred potential and catapulted me from restoring antiques to repairing human tissue.

Along the way, though, as I looked for inspiration, I began reading books by and about the people I most admired. I read about John Kennedy's prophecy of putting men on the moon. I read about William Wilberforce, Rosa Parks, the Wright brothers, and many other manifesters. As I examined the lives of these people, I saw that they had all begun by looking at the world around them, then looking within themselves until they discovered what they wanted passionately to accomplish. I recalled Benjamin Franklin, whose advice to his son was "You will never achieve anything unless you are enthusiastic about it." Looking up the etymology of *enthusiasm,* I discovered that it came from Greek roots that mean "having a god within." I realized that if I were ever to bring forth the special gifts that lay dormant within me and manifest the life of my dreams, I needed to be enthusiastic and inspired about my path.

And then, after I had finally discovered what I needed to be doing and was engaged in manifesting it, I learned that I had to be disciplined about bringing my dreams to fruition. As noted earlier, one of the medical doctors who shepherded me in realizing my goals taught me a basic principle of scientific method. Whenever you discover a new way of doing things, he said, it's essential to keep a detailed record of the process for two reasons: to leave a historical record and to create a road map so others can duplicate what you have done. So I began to document the results of the pioneering work we were doing and record the observations of the doctors with whom I worked.

I tried to keep the work under wraps until I was ready to present it in its fullness, but word got out. A friend of mine who knew about our work at the Global Health Institute showed special interest because she was having difficulty manifesting the change she wanted in her own life. A bright woman of Indian ancestry, Tamana had a successful career in internet technology but had come to a crossroads in her life. She held a good position at MTV but had been offered a job with a different company in San Diego. In the process of wrestling with this career decision, she asked if she could bounce some ideas off me. I agreed to meet her at the Mediterraneo Café, a great little place on Second Avenue. As we sat there sipping from steaming cappuccinos, Tamana sensed how excited I was that I had finally manifested the career of my dreams, and she wanted to know more. "How?" she kept asking. "How did you discover your path? How did you find your calling? How did you go about realizing the change you wanted to happen?"

"Hmm," I said, "let me see." I had followed a path, sure, but it wasn't until I looked back on it that the steps of that path became apparent, just as looking behind you at your tracks in the snow reveals the trail you've blazed through the woods. "I did it exactly the way all the great manifesters do," I said, "one step at a time."

Tamana looked at me expectantly. "Well," she said, "what ̀ the steps? What did you actually do?"

Until that moment I hadn't articulated the Five Steps. Ẁ out taking time to think about it logically, I allowed the visio of the great manifesters I had read about to wash over me an then let the steps flow out as I talked. "The first step," I said, "is t̀ look at the world around you and gather information. You look for the thing that registers in your heart, your gut, your intuition. It could be an idea for a new invention, or it could just be a pet peeve—say, that people are dumping garbage in a local park and nobody seems to care. Or it could be that you want to have a healthier life or to improve the way something is done at your job. Nothing is too small or too grand. Whatever it is, the key is to pay attention to the pearls of insight that your subconscious is trying to communicate to you."

I added that it didn't have to have anything to do with healing or healthcare. I love the saying of Teresa Hale, the Englishwoman who did so much to call attention to complementary medicine and founded the pioneering Hale Clinic in London: "Anything we do that helps the world is healing." That can apply to the environ-ment, healthcare, social justice, or technological invention.

I took another sip of my cappuccino and warmed to the story. "The next step," I said, "is to decide that you're going to do some-thing about it. Until you decide to make a change, it will remain an unrealized dream. But once you decide, you open the door."

"Oh," Tamana said, "just decide. That sounds easy. Almost *too* easy."

"Maybe," I said, "but it isn't. When you get ready to manifest a change in the world, just know this: It's the human condition to resist change. No matter what you want to transform, from the smallest improvement to the greatest evolution, there will be opposition. So you're going to need backup."

Tamana laughed and asked me what I meant.

"You probably won't be able to do it yourself," I said, "and by that I don't just mean that you'll need other people's help. You may or may not, that's beside the point. You'll need big-time support. I once heard a beautiful short quote that sums it all up: 'If you connect to a Higher Power, you'll be unstoppable.' This is a universal principle. All the world's cultures have words for the realm that we connect to, the force that is available to all of us. As you know, in India it's called *prana*."

"Yes," she said, "of course."

"In China they call it *chi*," I said, "and Western religions call it grace, believing that the ultimate Source is God. Now quantum physics describes this in completely secular, scientific terms. These scientists' studies show that a vast quantum field holds us all together in its invisible web, that we are in continuous contact with one another and with our environment, and that all kinds of unseen energy and information flow into us constantly and instantaneously. If we connect to that Source, we can achieve and manifest whatever we intend to do."

As I was weighing how much detail to give Tamana about my own experiences connecting to Source, I saw the other steps of the process fall into line in my mind's eye like pearls on a string. "The next step," I said, "is to act on your inspired decision. When you do that, the final step is to manifest the change you want—in yourself and the world.

"I define *acting* as 'intention in motion.' Martin Luther King had a dream. He looked around, saw what he needed to do, and decided to do something about it. He saw a nation complacent about the disease of racism, and to him this was unacceptable. Then he connected to Source—and if you've ever watched footage of King speaking, you can see how his eyes were lit by heavenly fire. Finally, he acted. He assembled thousands of people to march, first down South and then in Washington, D.C. And in doing so, he manifested enormous change in the world, change that is still manifesting."

Without further explanation, I called to Vito, the manager of the café, who happened to be nearby, and asked if he had a piece of paper I could use. He said no, but he handed me a napkin. Then and there, I wrote down these five steps: *Look. Decide. Connect. Act. Manifest.*

At that, I jumped up from my chair, left enough money to cover the bill, and apologized to Tamana. "Sorry," I blurted out, "I've got to go."

"Where are you going?" she asked, laughing.

"I'm so sorry," I said. "I have to go write all this down. Thanks for helping me verbalize my thoughts!"

Then I ran back to my apartment, got on my computer, and wrote down these steps where I wouldn't lose them. (I do still have the napkin, though.)

Now, when I look back at many of the landmarks in my personal story, I can see how they match up with one or more of the steps just as I outlined them to Tamana that day at Mediterraneo Café. In our lifetime we experience many small manifestations as well as larger ones. Writing a heartfelt letter can be a manifestation, just like resolving a problem at your workplace or within your life, discovering the cure for polio, ending a civil injustice, or putting people on the moon. Some changes can manifest in one day, while others can cover the course of a lifetime.

Likewise, the steps leading to manifestation of your dream may sometimes occur in a neat sequence, while at other times several steps may seem to happen at once, on top of one another or in rapid succession. What's most important is to keep sight of the overall process, so that if you feel blocked along your path, you can recognize which step you seem to be stuck on and then do what you need to get moving again. You can begin at the beginning with Step One, or, if you feel you're already engaged in the process, you can pick it up wherever you think you are.

The remainder of this book will spell out each of the Five Steps in detail and explain how you can adapt these steps to manifest the change you want to see in the world.

My dad, the iconic cowboy—
a real tough act to follow.

Visiting Dad at his firehouse. Mom is
holding me alongside Dad and Jake.

A 1959 Marlboro advertise-
ment. Inscribed, "To Jack—
The Marlboro Man, who never
changes," by the artist, Gustav
Rehberger. Illustration gift of
Gustav Rehberger.

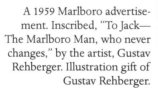

Me at age seven with my brother, Jake, Dad, and my sister, Cassie, on Cape Cod, Massachusetts.

The Smith Point lifesaving crew, the summer of the sinking camper rescue. I'm in the center row, fourth from the left.

Midshipman J. P. Farrell at the helm of the training ship *Empire State* while serving as a cadet in the U.S. Maritime Administration.

Looking for a teacher in all the wrong places: gazing at a portrait of J. P. Morgan.

A party memento from my former life: buying into the empty promise that more is better.

Fall to grace: restoring art and antiques while seeking a new course in life.

The broken church carving I was commissioned to restore—with newly fabricated replacement nose.

The church carving after my restoration.

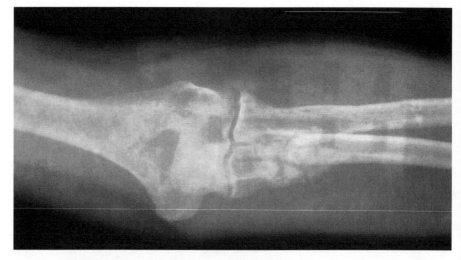

X-ray of Greg Sherman's arm showing multiple fractures.
Photo courtesy of Global Health Institute.

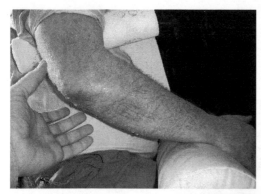

The mending of Greg's arm by
consciousness-based healthcare.
Photo courtesy of Global Health
Institute.

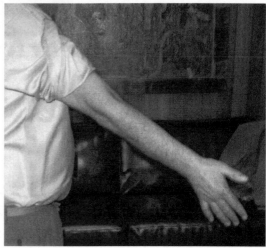

Greg's arm, completely healed.
Photo courtesy of Global
Health Institute.

As a surgeon observes, I demonstrate on Ellen Scarborough a spiritually based intervention to transform human tissue. Photo courtesy of Global Health Institute.

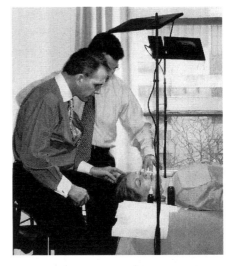

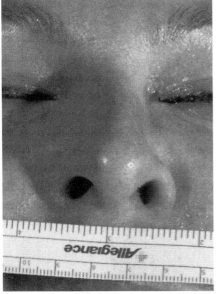

Ellen's nose tip lifted and narrowed. Photo courtesy of Global Health Institute.

Ellen described the result of my intervention as "like marble, polished marble." Photo courtesy of Global Health Institute.

Sammy at ten months old. By the time we met, Sammy was twenty and had undergone thirty-five surgeries.

SAMMY 10MONTHS

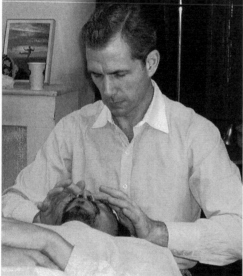

Removing scar tissue on Sammy's face.

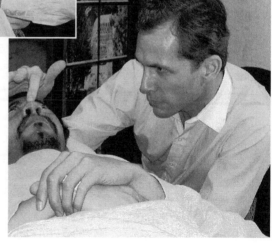

Restoring Sammy's nose.

**PRE**- Sammy before the intervention.

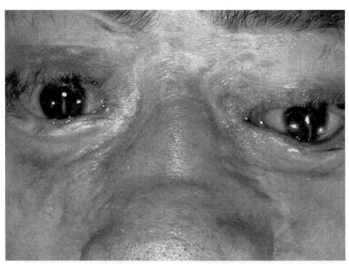

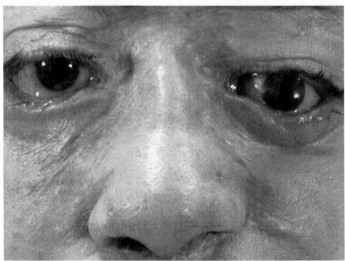

**POST**- Sammy one week after the intervention.

J.P. and Sammy,
friends for life!

Today I'm a teacher, lecturer, and researcher. Each morning I wake with immense gratitude that, despite my guidance counselor's advice, I acted anyway—and manifested a life beyond my wildest adult imagination.

Chapter 17

---

# STEP ONE: LOOK

We were born to make manifest the
glory of God that is within us. It's not
just in some of us; it's in everyone.
And as we let our own light shine, we
unconsciously give other people per-
mission to do the same. As we are liberated from our own fear, our presence
automatically liberates others.
　　　　—Marianne Williamson


What does it feel like to remember
your soul's task?
　　　　—Gary Zukav


Looking is the first step in discovering and unearthing your
uniqueness, passion, and sacred desires. As I define it, looking is
the process of receiving and gathering information. In this chapter you will find the necessary insight to gather information not

only with your eyes but also with your other senses. While sight, sound, taste, touch, and smell will yield abundant information in the process of discovery, only by looking inside and listening to the whispers of our hearts and the inner sensations that we so often ignore will we be able to identify our sacred inheritance.

As the old proverb goes, "The journey of a thousand miles begins beneath one's feet." That saying is sometimes stated "The journey of a thousand miles begins with the first step," but that's not quite accurate. You have to know where you are and the direction that you want to go in before you can take the first step in manifesting the life you were created for.

Some people coast through life, being directed by others or following the well-trod paths created for them. Others set sail with their destinies limited by the belief that our potential to succeed is determined by our parents, money, social status, or higher education. This is not true.

In past centuries around the world, it was common for the first-born to inherit the family wealth and land, while the other children were limited to entering the family business, learning a trade, or joining the military or clergy. Women's lives were even more rigidly laid out, limited for the most part to marriage and a narrow range of careers. With the inception of the women's rights movement, however, women have begun to progress rapidly and, in the United States and elsewhere, are surpassing men in college admissions and entry into professional careers and increasingly making their influence felt.

We are at the beginning of a new millennium, in which the false limits of our potential are being shattered, and the world is witnessing many firsts as humanity moves forward on its evolutionary path. As new ideas and lost sacred knowledge, such as the Law of Attraction and other spiritual principles, become more widely known, new horizons and possibilities in all areas of human endeavor seem within our reach. The whole nature of life is being transformed, so it's more crucial than ever to pay attention to what is going on around you.

As you embark on your path to ignite your sacred potential to manifest change, I want to make clear yet again that this is not an intellectual process. And realizing sacred potential is available to all, so don't be intimidated.

While I was writing this book, I spent days searching for a quotation to convey the idea that we all have been born with different gifts. I had no luck, but one day I went out to the local copy shop to print out an early draft of the manuscript. I was standing in line when the woman in front of me, her arms full of flyers and pamphlets, turned around and looked at me. It was kind of an odd moment; she hesitated and then asked me if I had any children in the Boy Scouts or Girl Scouts. I said no, but I thought they were good groups, and that I'd been a Scout as a child and enjoyed it.

Then she handed me a pamphlet. "I don't know why," she said, "but I just feel that you should have a copy of this." I couldn't think of any use I might have for a Cub Scout booklet, but to be polite I took it and put it in my pocket. On my way home, I stopped off at the neighborhood coffee shop, and while I was sipping my coffee, I pulled out the booklet to reminisce about my childhood scouting experiences. And it was there that I found the quotation I'd been looking for. The booklet's opening section was entitled "Developing Talents," and on the first page was this quotation:

> For all have not every gift given unto them;
> for there are many gifts,
> and to every one is given a gift
> by the spirit of God.

I was so glad that the woman in line before me had listened to her inner voice and for no logical reason acted on her guidance and gave me the pamphlet that contained the exact quotation that I was searching for.

The feelings that register within you—in your heart, throat, stomach—those unconscious clues will reveal to you your sacred purpose. Looking is the first step, but allowing those clues to register on your radar is part of that step. By listening to your inner signals and allowing your reactions to your environment, workplace, and family to register, and by paying attention to the message within, your sacred gift, the reason you were created for, will reveal itself to you. That sacred potential within you is your inheritance waiting to be claimed.

It's like a poor man who inherits a piece of property and spends his life chasing opportunities in his village and elsewhere without ever quite succeeding. The man dies in poverty, and on his death his daughter inherits the property. Then one day while she is digging in the soil in front of their home, the same ground that her father had trod every day of his life, she unearths a vast, unknown treasure.

Many of the world's spiritual traditions teach that each of us possesses a divine gift inside, a gift that we were born with. This gift takes many forms, and our task is to locate and identify our inner passions and dreams, because when we do that we will discover what we're supposed to be doing in life. Most people rely on their intellect or batteries of test questions to identify the role best suited for them. But our potential cannot be measured by a test or a process that is incapable of gauging the heart, soul, courage, or will.

This method of looking for your path is flawed, and many who stick to the course in life set by this method are unenthusiastic about their work, feeling disconnected and uninspired, and as a result never seem to bear fruit. More than anything, we need to feel enthused by what we do. I did not discover until I was forty that the path my guidance counselor set for me was way off the mark. As a result, the mistaken opportunities I pursued for years were the real reasons for my sadness. If I had listened to my sadness, I might have decided to transform my life earlier.

My mother is a wonderful cook, and often in the summer I watch her as she goes out to her garden to pick the perfect ingredients for her tomato sauce or salads. She doesn't rely on her intellect as she is making a selection. Instead, she relies on her senses of smell, and touch, and sight, and taste to discover the best produce. Archaeologists who go in search of priceless buried ruins have long trained themselves to look for a clue, a little sign indicating the promise of a hidden treasure. They call this a "tell."

So, as I learned from the woman I met in line at the copy shop, and others who have listened to their inner voices, we must heed all our senses and the wisdom of our emotions, because they may be trying to give us a valuable message. These feelings you get will help you to unearth your individual gifts. Listen to your heart and to what your gut is telling you. Sometimes you just inherently know that a path being recommended by others is wrong for you, regardless of how you measure up on paper. Don't be afraid to bloom. As Marianne Williamson put it, "Your playing small does not serve the world." Think big! And quite frankly, ignore those naysayers who don't really know you and can't possibly see the sacred potential that resides within you.

Be alert to whatever messages come to give you a clue from your soul to your true calling. The clue may arrive at any time and in the most unlikely place: sitting on a bus, walking or driving to work, watching television, taking a shower, or sitting on the john in the morning.

As the saying goes, sometimes you can't see the forest for the trees. To find your mission, you may have to look elsewhere, change your perspective. You may have to get off your normal path and abandon your usual routine. If you are swamped with stimuli and still your sacred purpose has not been revealed to you, you may need to find a place free from outside stimulation. Try eliminating the TV, radio, newspapers, and other input, so that you may look and listen within. If you live in a noisy city, maybe you need to head for stillness. Spend time in the country, at a beach, in the mountains, or just go and sit in a quiet place, like a house of worship or a museum. I love the saying that I have on my desk, "Sometimes it is only when the mind is still and we are quiet, that we can receive sacred guidance."

On the other hand, if you already live in a quiet, serene environment, you may need to connect to the outside world in some way. There's a wonderful story of a group of people traveling from New York City to a secluded Buddhist temple in search of spiritual answers. When they arrived at the temple and were shown around, they were dismayed to see the monks reading *The New York Times*. "Why are you reading the newspaper?" one of the visitors asked.

"We are isolated in a temple," the head monk replied. "We need to gather information so we know what to pray for."

Listen to your inner voice and to the knowledge your body is sending you. We've all had feelings register within us, felt choked up or sick to our stomachs. Many people have experienced heartache from a loss or felt tremendous love or empathy in their hearts.

I hope I've made it clear that your eyes are not the only organs with which you can "see." The less you rely only on your eyes, the more your other senses will be heightened. As we lose the ability to receive information from one sense, our other senses become more powerful. Anyone who has ever had the privilege of watching blind musicians such as Stevie Wonder or Ray Charles create great music can attest to that. In the Far East, it has long been known that blind people make the best massage therapists because they are capable of sensing tension, disease, and stress with their hands better than sighted people can.

Science is just discovering that we have sensory abilities that cannot be explained or measured by the current level of technology. Most people acknowledge that a mother has an innate connection with her children, and this is true with animals too. They have abilities to sense and gather messages that we as humans lack or have lost, given our reliance on our dominant senses of sight and sound.

The tsunami that devastated Southeast Asia in 2004 was one of the worst disasters in history. But just before the tsunami hit the coastlines, a herd of working elephants that had been chained near the sea acted in unison, much to the confusion of their handlers. The great beasts began breaking free from their shackles and, for no reason apparent to their human overseers, marched to higher ground. Elephants have special bones in their feet that enable them to sense seismic vibrations long before we can. They listened to their senses and were able to avoid approaching danger, saving themselves from the massive wave that came ashore moments later and took such a huge toll in human life.

My favorite role model for someone who listened to her inner voice, and so discovered the appropriate decision to act, is Rosa Parks. Rosa was a woman of color who was not born with the markings of a leader. No test could have ever predicted her potential for greatness, yet she left a legacy that has benefited the generations that followed. When Rosa got out of bed on that day in December 1955 when she refused to give up her seat on the bus, she had no idea that she was about to set in motion a chain of events that would transform the nation. Rosa had been humiliated on previous occasions by the segregated bus system of Montgomery, Alabama, where she worked. She was active in the local NAACP and had discussed ways to call attention to the injustices of segregation. But the essential truth of her cause was revealed to her by simply listening to the wisdom and inherent sense of justice in her soul, and acting on the higher truth percolating into her conscious mind. Rosa acted against the law of the local government but in line with divine law. It was a time when people of color were made to sit in the back of the bus and, if the whites-only section in front filled up, even to give up their seats in the colored section. Rosa had experienced indignity before but, as we all do, had learned to suppress her outrage until she could not anymore.

And with that simple inner knowing and the small action of one woman, a huge step for humanity began in Alabama and spread throughout the country. Rosa Parks's soul set out on a path she was intended to take. Being arrested and going to jail for challenging the unjust law was better to her than quietly bearing one more act of abuse.

Sensing injustice with her heart, Rosa set off a manifestation of change on a grand scale. Your calling may have nothing to do with large social causes. What you see that needs to change may seem like a small thing, but it will be an important clue in your life. Listen to the wisdom of your heart, and keep an internal ear open to the messages percolating up in your soul. Discovering your sacred calling will transform your life and, just maybe, the world.

## Chapter 18

##### STEP TWO: DECIDE

When making a decision of minor importance, I have always found it advantageous to consider all the pros and cons. In vital matters, however, such as the choice of a partner or a profession, the decision should come from the unconscious, from somewhere within ourselves. In the important decisions of personal life, we should be governed, I think, by the deep inner needs of our nature.

—Sigmund Freud

You will either step forward into growth, or you will step backward into safety.

—Abraham Maslow

Once you find the groove, make the decision, commit to it and follow through.

—Paul Berguson

When I was a midshipman at the maritime college, I used to volunteer in the medical corpsman's office. I watched the physicians work, and I learned some of the simplest tasks, like how to take blood pressure, use salves to treat burns, change dressings, bandage sprains, and dispense salt tablets for heat exhaustion. I thought medicine was a noble profession, but my involvement in it was minor at best. In the summer of 1988, I was involved in business, because, as I've already noted, my high school guidance counselor had told me that, on paper, I didn't have the potential to follow my dream of working in healthcare and helping people. In my childish eyes, he was a person of authority. Coming from a family of policemen and firefighters, all of whom had been in the military in their youth, I was trained to respect authority and follow orders. That may work well in the military (although not always), and there is nothing inherently wrong with authority figures. But as my soul was rebelling against the course I was following, a chance encounter with another authority figure helped me see how wrong my guidance counselor had been. I began to look at the course of my life and to know, deep inside, that it was time to make a decision to get my life back on its true track.

I was about twenty-eight at the time, working in real estate brokerage by day and studying real estate investment at Pace University in the evenings. In between I donated some of my time to serve on the board of the Soldiers', Sailors', Marines', Coast Guard & Airmen's Club. They own a building on Lexington Avenue near Thirty-sixth Street that offers rooms to service members at greatly reduced rates. We were getting ready for a fund-raiser when, after hanging decorations and climbing ladders much of the day, I met a friend of one of the members, a man named Paul Berguson. When Paul asked me what I was doing there, I laughed and told him that I'd been shanghaied into helping out. I learned that he was a doctor and professor at the NYU School of Medicine, several blocks away. I told him how I had originally wanted to study healthcare but had abandoned my dream at my counselor's recommendation. I added that I had worked as a medical corpsman and loved every minute of it. "I think it must be great being able to help people and ease their suffering," I said. "So, Paul, what made you decide to be a doctor?"

"I grew up on a dairy farm in Mansfield, Pennsylvania," he said, "and one day when I was a young teenager, the tractor attachment became stuck. I pushed it with my hip, and it bounced off and landed on me, crushing my leg and hip." Paul said he nearly died and spent most of the next year in the hospital. One day he asked for something to read, and his doctor gave him a copy of the *Merck Manual*, a thick tome listing just about every disease and ailment know to medicine. "Here," the doctor said, "read this, and when you leave here you'll know about as much as any doctor does."

Paul read the manual cover to cover, along with the other books he could get his hands on, making a pest out of himself by asking the doctors and nurses questions. He quickly realized that they were not omniscient, and that he could learn as much as and more than they knew. That was when he decided that he was going to be a doctor. Reflecting on the tone of regret he must have picked up from my own story, he added rather kindly, "It's not too late to go to med school, Joseph."

I appreciated his gesture, but I also felt overwhelmed at the prospect. "Even if I wanted to study medicine," I said, "I can't imagine what that would be like."

"Well," Dr. Berguson replied, "how would you like to spend a day in med school?"

I thought he was joking. "What do you mean?"

"How would you like to trail me as I make my rounds at the medical school this Saturday?"

"Really?" I said, with childlike excitement.

"Sure," he said. "With your student medical corpsman background, I see no reason why you couldn't trail me on rounds as a potential candidate for med school. After all, we'll be at a teaching university, and we have nurses, EMTs, and physician's assistants learning there as they go. There's a saying: 'Watch one, do one, teach one.' You never know what you might pick up!"

We agreed to meet at 8:30 on Saturday at a deli near Gramercy Park. When I arrived, Dr. Berguson was waiting, coffee in hand, dressed in a pair of funny clogs and loose-fitting pants. As we walked across the street, I realized what an imposing figure he cut, a big, stout man with the demeanor of Henry VIII and a curly, reddish beard. To my mind, Paul was the essence of what a medical professor should look like, and when he walked it was more like a march than a simple stroll. I had to double-time just to keep up. We hustled through the corridors and into a locker room, where he hung up his street clothes, tossed me some blue scrubs, and told me to change.

When I was ready, he said that we'd begin. "I'm a professor of anesthesiology," he said. "And what do anesthesiologists do? They keep the patients alive while surgeons are operating." He explained that anesthesiology is a relatively new field. "Just a hundred years ago," he said, "there was no anesthesia. Not only was surgery very painful but many surgeries couldn't even be performed because patients in such pain move too much."

As Dr. Berguson spoke, we were busily scrubbing our hands, turning the water off with our elbows. He put a pair of latex gloves on my hands and a surgical mask on my face, giving it a quick pinch around the nose so it fit snugly. I was a bit anxious, but being around such a consummate professional imbued me with faith. "Don't say anything, don't touch anything," Paul said. "Just observe."

We spent the first part of the morning observing five surgeries that were going on simultaneously. Berguson greeted each team of surgeons and anesthesiologists by name, explaining that he had a medical student candidate trailing today. We went from a hand surgery to a knee to heart bypass. I stood back five feet, looking on in utter awe as one surgeon removed a heart and held it in his hand while another surgeon was removing a vessel from the patient's leg to be used to bypass the defective arteries. Although I'd been advised to stand still and observe, the surgeon told me to step closer. I hesitated, but he kept urging me closer until I was standing at the patient's shoulder and found myself looking down—into the open chest cavity.

And then I felt it, a wave of unruly energy rising from the pit of my stomach and spreading up my throat and over my scalp. I rocked involuntarily on my heels as the wave traveled its course, then just as suddenly found my footing again. It was like finding your sea legs on a moving ship with a rolling wave passing under the hull. The surgeon handed me a penlike, stainless steel object attached to a wire and told me to hold it. He was using it to cauterize little capillaries that were sprouting in the inner chest. Then he took it back from me and continued the process with astounding dexterity.

After that I observed a young girl whose spine was being straightened by implanting a metal rod called a Harrington rod. It was developed in the 1950s by Paul Harrington and was a major advance in the treatment of scoliosis.

Later, as we tossed our latex gloves into the trash, Dr. Berguson announced that we'd be attending grand rounds. He explained that during this time the senior doctors question the residents and interns on their patients and proposed treatment protocols. At one point he led me into the private room of a woman who had had ankle surgery. She was under a sheet and asked who it was in an oddly familiar, quavering voice. When Paul announced himself, the woman pulled away the sheet, revealing herself to be Katharine Hepburn. Dr. Berguson introduced me as a potential student, and she was as gracious as could be. He had obviously helped her a great deal, and she invited both of us to come to dinner at her town house on Forty-ninth Street, where we later did go.

I was thinking that put a perfect cap on the day's excitement, but as we were heading down the hall to the physicians' locker room, we encountered a nurse talking with a very agitated family just outside a room. Three women, who appeared to be mother, daughter, and grandchild, were very distraught as elevated voices emanated from the room. Dr. Berguson stopped and conferred with the nurse, who reported that the interns were trying without success to insert a breathing tube. Paul turned to me and said he would just be a minute. Like Clark Kent disappearing into a phone booth, he dashed into the room and took charge of the situation.

From the hallway I could hear Paul's authoritative voice calmly instructing the interns precisely how to find the proper angle to insert the tube. He was clearly showing them how it was done. "Once you find the groove," he said, "make the decision, commit to it, and follow through in one motion."

Meanwhile, the family were eyeing me expectantly. In my blue scrubs and with a surgical mask dangling from my neck, I must have looked like a doctor to them. Since I was not a medical professional, however, it wasn't my place to offer advice or an opinion. Yet I empathized with their situation, and it suddenly came to me how I could help. "You're very lucky," I said to them. "The man who just walked into that room is an expert. He wrote the book on anesthesiology, and he teaches other doctors how to perform these procedures. I'm sure he'll sort it out in just a minute. You're fortunate that he happened to be passing by."

With that they all smiled and visibly relaxed. In another moment, Dr. Berguson came out, turning on his heels while talking to the nurse. The three women looked at him with great reverence. "Thank you, Doctor," they said, virtually in unison as Paul nodded. As we continued on our way to the locker room, Paul expressed mild surprise at the outpouring of thank-yous. "What was that all about?" he said.

"I told them that you were the big dog," I said, smiling. "That you're the professor and they were lucky to have you stroll by."

As we walked and talked, he gave me a curious look. "I think you may have missed your calling," he said at last. "You would make an excellent doctor."

In retrospect, I can't help recalling the words Dr. Berguson spoke to the interns in that room: "Once you find the groove, make the decision, commit to it, and follow through in one motion." I know he was talking about a medical procedure, and a relatively simple one at that. But what he said also applies to the next step on the path to realizing your sacred potential.

I learned several important lessons from my one-day visit to medical school, but they all boil down to the simple teaching method that Dr. Berguson had mentioned to me earlier: "Watch one, do one, teach one." The method, popular in medical schools, gives students the opportunity to observe, practice, and explain a medical procedure. These different ways of learning help us to understand and remember the procedures we need to know. Your mind learns to break down the steps of a process, first by observing and learning visually; then by practicing hands-on; and finally by internalizing the process so that you can teach it to others. As we know, teaching is the best way of expanding our own knowledge and understanding. As we search our minds and hearts for ways to explain what we are doing—through examples and parables, as the great spiritual masters have always taught—we see the process with greater depth and precision.

As Freud said, your decision to find your true calling should ultimately come from your subconscious. You may involve your rational mind in weighing options or figuring out the details, but the main thrust of your decision has to come from deep within. Lots of books and career gurus tell us to watch the economy, for example, to discover where the growth is at the moment, and then get on the bandwagon. But that's often like trying to fit your personality into a preconceived profile, your square peg into a round hole.

When I say your most crucial decisions should come from your subconscious mind, that doesn't mean you should wait for a mystical vision of some kind. That might be nice, but you could be waiting a long time. Your subconscious speaks to you in a number of ways, most of which you can train yourself to become aware of and take action on. The most obvious examples are your emotional responses to people and events. That day of med school moved me on so many levels—none of them really intellectual despite all the medical knowledge I was exposed to—that the end result was a deeply spiritual decision to pursue my life's dream after all. I was impressed by Dr. Berguson's self-assurance, his ability to take charge of a situation the way a ship's commander might. But he was also generous with me and considerate to just about everyone he came in contact with. More than anything, though, I saw the relief in the faces of those women when Paul came to the rescue of that patient about whom they cared so much.

That day reawakened in me the dream of restoring people's lives that had been snuffed by a misguided guidance counselor all those years before. I decided then and there that I would pursue the dream again. I may not have been fully conscious of my decision, but it had been made. Other events would conspire to push me in that direction, until I really had no choice but to quit my senseless job selling real estate.

The significance of some experiences that shape our lives isn't immediately apparent. When I "just happened" to start chatting with Paul Berguson at the Soldiers', Sailors', Marines', Coast Guard & Airmen's Club that day, I had no idea that he was a professor at a medical school. Once I found out and shared my repressed dream of working in healthcare, I still didn't think of the meeting as anything more than an interesting coincidence. But looking back on that day, I see that it had an important impact on my future. Finally, there was the chance encounter in the hospital hallway with the anxious family of a patient, which I can no more see as a coincidence than my initial encounter with Dr. Berguson.

So once you start paying attention to your subconscious or strong emotional responses to people and events, what do you do? First, see if these messages connect back to some wish or desire for change that you discovered while working on Step One. After you look—inside and outside yourself, as we discussed in the previous chapter—you will probably identify one or more areas for possible change, either in yourself or in the larger world. Indeed, the two may well be interrelated: Discovering your inner truth and igniting your sacred potential not only will make you a more fulfilled person but may also change the world in some small or large way.

One of the best examples of this relationship is the story of William Wilberforce (1759–1833), a British politician and philanthropist. Like most people in England at the time, Wilberforce pretty much accepted the slave trade as a necessary part of commerce. From a wealthy merchant family, he had no reason to question the status quo. His family could afford to send him to Cambridge, where Wilberforce was dismayed by the dissolute lives of his fellow students. But in 1785 he underwent a transformative experience, deciding to commit his life to service. Wilberforce became interested in social reform, and looking around him, he saw the slave trade with new eyes. After encountering a group of activists opposed to slavery, he took up the cause and became one of the leading English abolitionists. Several years before his conversion, Wilberforce had been elected to Parliament, ideally situating him to lead the fight to change the laws. He spent the next twenty-six years campaigning against the British slave trade, culminating in the passage of the Slave Trade Act of 1807.

Wilberforce's struggle was all the more difficult because most of his fellow members of Parliament were heavily invested in the slave trade and stood to lose a prime source of income if it were abolished. But he stuck with it. The decision Wilberforce made to go against the grain was certainly not an intellectual one; it wasn't what we'd call today a good career move. Yet having seen the inhumane treatment of slaves, he felt in his heart the heartlessness of the very idea of slavery. His personal decision to devote his life to noble service led directly to his fight against the slave trade, which made a huge impact on British society.

So once you've looked and decided on your particular calling or passion, it's time to do something about it. To act effectively, however, you will need support—and that's where the next step comes into play.

# Chapter 19

STEP THREE: CONNECT

The spiritual wayfarer gives herself to
her inner work and outer service.
                    —Llewellyn Vaughn-Lee


Only connect! That was the whole of
her sermon. Only connect the prose and
the passion, and both will be exalted, and
human love will be seen at its height.
                    —E. M. Forster


Let parents bequeath to their children
not riches but the spirit of reverence.
                    —Plato


We are all born with the ability to connect to a higher power,
sometimes called Source, Creator, the Field, the Divine—call it
what you will, God doesn't really care. Marianne Williamson

clearly captured this truth in *A Return to Love* when she wrote, "We are all meant to shine, as children do. We were born to make manifest the glory of God that is within us. It's not just in some of us: it's in everyone."

When I was a child, I thought like a child, and dreamed as a child with limitless possibilities, and knew things that I couldn't explain. I could manifest things so naturally, in fact, that it all seemed like child's play. But once I was enrolled in public school, I was reconditioned with new ideas, full of limits, clouded with a material worldview. And during that time it seemed that the joy and mystical component of my childhood were lost like sand falling through my fingers.

Not until years later, while sitting in the quiet of my basement studio, just permitting myself the luxury of once again imagining and dreaming with the limitless mind that I possessed as a child, was my heart's desire able to rise up and knock on the door to the unseen. And the Divine responded so enthusiastically that I was given the capacity to do the work that I held privately in my heart. I hadn't enrolled in any school program, hadn't traveled to any mountaintop, hadn't sat at the feet of any guru. I discovered the portal by remembering how to imagine like a child, igniting an unknown potential that catapulted me into a life beyond my wildest adult dreams.

As I look back at that experience, I realize it is not so much that we need to learn a whole new skill set to ignite our sacred capacity to manifest but instead that our capacity exists within each of us right now. We need to forget so we can remember.

Albert Einstein, one of the most brilliant men of the past century, said (and forgive me if I've quoted him before), "The most beautiful and profound emotion we can experience is the sensation of the mystical." It is the source of all true science, but it is not limited to science. Musicians from Wolfgang Amadeus

Mozart to John Coltrane have not been shy to give credit where credit is due. But what is the best way to ignite the sacred capacity that lies like a priceless inheritance within us?

To begin, we have to take charge of our own lives while drawing strength for our lives' missions by connecting to a higher Source. That may sound simple, but the obvious question is How? How do I connect to Source? Let me explain first by talking about my own experience, and then by saying a little about how other people connect. My hope is that while reading this chapter you will allow some words to penetrate you until, like tiny seeds, they take root and begin to grow the wisdom that will allow you to find your personal path to connecting.

When I was a midshipman, I went scuba diving in oceans around the world, surfed big waves in Hawaii, flew fast helicopters, and parachuted into the atmosphere to float down to Earth in absolute quiet. But the excitement of these distractions pales in comparison to harnessing the transformative power of the Sacred. When I first experienced a connection to Source, I wasn't really sure what was happening or how it had come about. I was vividly aware of my desire to open my heart to my longtime dream of helping other people, but I had no idea how to accomplish that. The only explanation I have is that I was being guided, that once I opened my heart and expressed the intention to help, God and the universe took over and led me on the path. It became clear to me from this experience and from talking to countless people who have shared their experiences with me that the road connecting to the Divine is a two-way street.

I have since had time to reflect on the process of connecting to Source that I go through, and, as a doctor will tell you, by watching, doing, and teaching, you gain a deeper understanding of the process. The most important thing to keep in mind is this: that the journey to connect to Source is not an intellectual pursuit. *You don't connect through your intellect.* Perhaps that's why most academics have been handicapped in their efforts to connect, while indigenous peoples and artists do it so easily. Connection is not a mental act; it is an act of surrender and of will, an invitation to the Divine to work through you.

As you play with uncovering the ability to feel the divine connection, I have found that it's helpful to remove stimuli that may preoccupy your body's senses. I like to connect to or, as some say, commune with the Divine closeted in the quiet of a small room, where I can limit external stimuli and cultivate the inner senses that allow us to get in touch with the Presence. At this point it is always good to forgive and let go of any resentment you may feel toward any person, institution, or circumstance that you believe has hurt or limited you. A heart occupied with hate and lower intentions cannot serve as a conduit for the Divine. Just as laughter cannot exist when anger is present, or light cannot exist where there is darkness, the Divine will not exist in a heart that is hardened or possessed by anger. In the East there is a saying: "Truly do I exist in all beings, but I am most manifest in man. The human heart is my favorite dwelling place."

One way to begin opening the heart center is by sending out feelings of gratitude for all that you have received. This practice makes you more available to receive grace, which flows into your heart and the whole of your being. As the force of grace flows into you, you feel love, and that love expands until you feel compassion for those around you. That can include someone who needs healing, or a social or political situation that needs to change.

Again, the way you generate compassion is not by thinking about it but by permitting yourself to feel empathy for others, friend and foe alike. Many people have had the experience of being in a room when someone who is at peace enters and the room begins to feel lighter.

Since 2000, I have done what I call my sacred practice every morning. And if I'm in a rush, to get to the airport or to the hospital, I take just a minute to acknowledge the connection until it expands and reaches the periphery of my physical body, which is the skin. Once you allow the sensation of spirit to push through there, you will discover that beyond the epidermis is a wider sheath of force that surrounds us. It's a little hard to describe the feeling in words; the whole process of spiritual expansion or mystical experience was characterized by the great American psychologist William James as *ineffable,* by which he meant that it is incapable of being defined or expressed verbally.

So you allow your heart to swell until it expands to the ineffable presence of the Divine, and in that moment you are connected to the Divine—again, call it Source, the universe, a Higher Power, or whatever name you prefer. In that moment you may experience Oneness with the divine Force. When I first had the experience of connecting, I was overcome with a feeling of peace, and all of the resentment I had accumulated through the years just vanished. It was beautiful, although I couldn't put it into words at the time, because it was also . . . ineffable.

At that point, I'm no longer doing anything. I may focus my attention on the person in front of me, or on the area of the body the person wants to change. But I'm not making anything happen. I become a conduit and surrender to a higher power. Thoughts, intentions, and actions imbued with and supercharged by the Divine can alter emotional as well as physical bodies. Probably the hardest part of this process for most of us to understand is not becoming a conduit to the Divine but allowing heart-to-heart empathy to form with a complete stranger. One day after I gave a talk in Texas, a lawyer took me to a sports bar to discuss what happens when I connect. A waitress with a bikini top came to take our orders. I was a bit taken by surprise; although it was just part of a costume, she didn't seem comfortable with it. As she took our orders, she looked into my eyes, and I allowed my heart to swell with a strong feeling of empathy for her. I held the intention that she would find something else to do, a higher and better purpose. A moment later her expression changed and she broke out sobbing, put the tray down, and ran out of the bar with a denim coat on.

The next day she tracked me down at the conference center where I was speaking and told me that she was a single mom and needed the extra money she earned at the sports bar to cover her car payments. But at that moment she had decided that she couldn't serve burgers and beverages in a bathing suit anymore. She told me she was going back to a local school to pursue a career she had always wanted: to become a paralegal.

The process of working with others from the heart instead of the mind is new to most in the West. Yet this skill is known by all of the great animal trainers. Animals have an innate ability to sense love and know who they can trust. One day when I was sitting on the end of a dock in the Florida Keys, a dolphin swam up to me and stayed suspended with its massive head out of the water so it could see me. I looked deeply into its eye, feeling that this was no dumb mammal but an intelligent, sentient being. Then I began apologizing for what humans were doing to its friends and its home. It was a profound experience for me, whether or not the message got through. Try sending love and empathy to a dog or horse; look the animal in the eye, allow your empathy to extend to it, and hold a thought or intention of love and concern.

In the West we spend most of our time and energy operating from our thinking mind. The Chinese say that where the mind goes, the life force will follow. "All mental states have mind as their forerunner, mind is their chief, and they are mind-made," the Buddha said some 2,500 years ago. "If one speaks or acts with a pure mind, happiness follows one as one's shadow that never leaves." The recent developments in science that I discussed in Chapter 10 have shown that we are constantly emitting energy, and that our energy affects the molecules of what we look at and whatever we focus our attention on. But attention is not the same as thinking.

By working so much of the time with words and the intellect, we have allowed our inner capacities to atrophy. But individuals who devote some practice to developing their inner strength, their ability to focus their attention, can learn to improve this innate capacity. Caroline Myss, author of *Anatomy of the Spirit* and *Sacred Contracts,* likes to say that intuition is not a special gift some people are born with; it's an *ability* we all have, and, as with any ability, we can develop and improve it with practice.

I remember as a child watching Martin Luther King speaking on television. Even at that young age I could see that as he delivered his orations—alternately somber and rousing—he was completely imbued with inner light, inner fire. I knew that his full name was the Rev. Dr. Martin Luther King, Jr., but I'm not sure I realized until later that he was a pastor as well as a political visionary. Now when I watch the videos of King's speeches, not only can I see the light in his eyes but I also hear in his voice the cadence of a preacher inspired by the Divine. That divine energy flowing through King not only empowered him and his followers but also rippled out to millions of people in the United States and around the world.

How did Dr. King connect to Source? Well, we know that he prayed, that he sang and listened to gospel music in church. So when you want to begin developing the capacity to empower your life and actions and words with the support of the Divine, you may find it helpful to spend some time practicing prayer.

One of the positive developments of the past century has been the dissemination of mystical wisdom once restricted to initiates of particular religions. Through a combination of world events and a general opening from within the traditions, we can now study not only the teachings but also the experiential rituals of Kabbalah, Zen and Tibetan Buddhism, mystical Islam, Native American spirituality, shamanism, Taoism, hatha yoga, and much more. Just sixty or seventy years ago, it would have been virtually impossible for most laypeople in the West to participate in a Native American sweat lodge, practice Christian meditation or centering prayer, study Kabbalistic wisdom, engage in Sufi dancing, or learn advanced forms of yoga and qigong. Now we can do all of those and more.

If you're interested in learning the basics of meditation, to get your feet wet before moving to more profound dimensions, you can choose one of the secular versions of some of these practices that are widely taught for the purpose of stress reduction, such as insight meditation, which is now used by many hospitals and behavioral health centers. Herbert Benson, the Harvard physician and teacher, based his highly regarded relaxation response on meditation practices derived from India. Benson himself was skeptical at first, but after performing his own studies, he was astonished to discover that practitioners could lower their blood pressure and heart rate simply by breathing deeply and rhythmically and repeating an ordinary word. He determined that you can silently repeat any word—such as *love, peace, hope, one,* or *yes*—and achieve stress reduction. Since he published his groundbreaking book *The Relaxation Response* in 1975, many other physicians and scientists have verified the beneficial effects of this kind of meditation.

Dr. James Gordon has pointed out that classic meditation developed during the long agricultural era of history, when people had much less to do and sitting still in silence was commonplace. The deeper truth is that meditation can take many forms and doesn't have to be limited to the formal methods I've mentioned, religious or secular. My mother loves gardening, for instance, and she often says that it is her favorite form of meditation. "When I'm gardening," she once told me, "all of my material, day-to-day concerns go out the window. That's a time when my soul is quieted." I know lots of people who engage in activities that take their minds off their daily concerns and allow them to experience extended moments of peace. These can include knitting, whittling, beading, painting, ironing, listening to music, or walking in the woods. These pursuits often unconsciously open people to receiving support from the Source. When Obi-Wan Kenobi teaches Luke Skywalker to use "the Force" in the Star Wars films, he is talking about something akin to the Chinese concept of the Tao, the mystical force of life underlying the universe. If we can tap into the Tao, then the Force is with us.

Many masters of qigong and tai chi teach their students how to draw on "cosmic" energy that is constantly being generated in the depths of the universe. And once again, that practice is supported by recent scientific studies that indicate energy is always flowing around us and among us. As one teacher used to say, it's a little like listening to the radio. Radio waves surround you wherever you are, containing all kinds of broadcasts; all you need is a receiver tuned to the proper frequency to pick them up.

The ancient discipline of tai chi is often referred to as a moving meditation. One day I was practicing this exercise outdoors at dusk. The sun had descended behind a building, leaving the wall twenty feet in front of me dark and a perfect backdrop. My left hand, palm up, was sweeping like a moving cloud away from my body. I could see a visible mist of energy vibrating and floating in the wake of my hand like a large, iridescent jellyfish. At such moments, your inner life force expands beyond yourself—even if you can't see it. In their paintings and frescoes, the old masters often depicted the heads and bodies of spiritual seekers surrounded by auras, or circular halos of light. Those auras weren't just cute decorative devices (although they have sometimes been reduced to that). They were meant to show what some people could see—the light flowing from the Source to beings who walked the earth or emanating from their own bodies.

A person imbued with scientific theories at the dawn of the twentieth century would have considered flight impossible and space travel limited to the realm of science fiction. Even today it is difficult to understand the words of a teacher who instructed his followers two thousand years ago, "I tell you with certainty, if you have faith and do not doubt . . . you will also say to this mountain, 'Be removed and thrown into the sea,' and it will happen." He was talking not about religious faith or dogma but simply about believing that what you intend will come to be. When Wayne Dyer wrote a book entitled *You'll See It When You Believe It*, he was playing on the old axiom "I'll believe it when I see it." By turning this saying on its head, Dyer was pointing out that we first have to believe we are spiritual beings having a physical experience—not the reverse—to realize that the things we mistakenly consider impossible are just dreams we haven't yet manifested. I love the saying "Miracles don't create believers, believers create miracles." When we truly believe, without a speck of doubt, that we can manifest the change we want in the world, we will start seeing it.

We must also realize that we are not isolated beings. If we can reconnect with the force that created us, and draw lifeblood from the umbilical cord that we believe was cut but actually wasn't, then we can be at one with everything. The way we can do that is by learning to feel that life force or grace flowing through us.

Once you acknowledge the force and begin to play with it, you can master it and use it for many things. One of those uses, of course, could be healing individuals of physical ailments. But you can use the same force for healing social ills or the body politic, changing where you live or the kind of work you do.

While it's helpful to have friends or a community of like-minded souls who are a bit more enlightened, we also have to share this knowledge with those who most need change in their lives. The Sufi teacher and author Llewellyn Vaughn-Lee has said that we don't have to bring the message of personal and global transformation into the yoga studios and New Age seminars and workshops where people already know about it. This is called preaching to the choir. We have to bring it into the places of power and into the boardrooms of greedy, self-absorbed people, because they need this healing more than the conscious person does. Lynne Twist wrote in her book *The Soul of Money* that excess wealth can be an obstacle to happiness. "Mother Teresa taught me that wealth is no protection from human suffering, and I have seen it firsthand in my own work," Twist says. Many of the world's most wealthy people live trapped in a cage of privilege, in which material comforts are plentiful, but spiritual and emotional deprivation are real and painful. Often the wealthy suffer from loneliness and isolation, especially when so many relationships are all about money and lack the genuine qualities of love or friendship." This doesn't mean that you have to take a vow of poverty. As a wise teacher once said, "Seek first the kingdom of heaven, and all this [meaning material well-being] will be added to you."

As I said earlier, there are many ways to connect to the Source. You can find the one that works best for you and work with it until you develop some basic mastery. You should then try to practice it as often as you can, once a day if possible. Use this practice when you focus on the kind of change you want to manifest, in your life and in the world. After a while you will become supported in your work in whatever field of human endeavor you are engaged. To paraphrase the poet Rumi, beyond the limits and restraints of the materialist worldview is a field where all is possible. I will meet you there.

# Chapter 20

STEP FOUR: ACT

Conditions are never just right. People
who delay action until all factors are
favorable are the kind who do nothing.
—William Feather

You don't need to see the top of the
stairs to take the first step in faith.
—Martin Luther King, Jr.

I felt called to do what I call "get in the
way," to be maladjusted.
—John Lewis

Once you've established the connection with the Divine I described
in the previous chapter, you're ready to act. It says in Proverbs, "As
a man thinks in his heart, so shall he be." Our "thoughts"—which
in this context include intentions and feelings, the expansion of

the heart beyond the physical body—create chain reactions in the external world. To act means to put your decision into motion, because a decision is like a seed in the ground: Unless you water it, tend to it, nurture it, and keep the pests away, it will never grow into anything. Decisions not acted on manifest nothing. Even the most experienced of meditators eventually have to get up off the cushion and act on their practice.

But you may wonder why you should act at all. Why not just stay in your room and think, or pray, or meditate, or practice yoga, or read comic books?

The best reason of all is what is sometimes called enlightened self-interest, a principle that may have been first identified by Alexis de Tocqueville, the French political thinker and historian who visited America in 1831. He observed that Americans were "fond of explaining almost all the actions of their lives by the principle of self-interest rightly understood; they show . . . how an enlightened regard for themselves constantly prompts them to assist one another."

I would put that slightly differently: Not only does the world need change but so do you. Each of us has to identify the divine gift within to feel fulfilled on a deep level. According to Deepak Chopra, "We are divinity in disguise, and the gods and goddesses in embryo that are contained within us seek to be fully materialized. True success is therefore . . . the unfolding of divinity within us." Our true nature, the sacred inheritance I have talked about throughout this book, is what we need to bring forth so that we can identify with it and live lives that are aligned with who we are on the deepest level. By doing that, we not only make ourselves happier and more fulfilled but also spread that happiness to everyone around us, our families, friends, colleagues, and the rest of the world on which we focus our attention.

The second reason for acting out our decisions to manifest

change is, of course, to repair the world, or what is called in the Jewish tradition *tikkun olam*. The world needs repair and improvement in every field of human endeavor. There is no shortage of transformational work that has to be done to bring our planet into the Light, to take it to what the Jesuit priest and paleontologist Pierre Teilhard de Chardin called the Omega Point—the highest level of complexity and consciousness toward which the universe appears to be evolving.

But the only way change is going to happen is if you act on your decisions. We certainly can't wait for institutions to save the world for us. It's up to us to bring forth our inspired solutions, whether they be in technology, education, politics, energy, environmentalism, or art.

The world is improving one bold step at a time. When I was a child, segregation was still a blatant fact of life in my own country and elsewhere. In this world, women had fewer rights than men and could not expect to rise above a certain level in many fields of work. It was also a world where people thought virtually nothing of driving around drunk and risking the lives of other motorists and pedestrians, until a few angry mothers got organized, said enough is enough, and acted for change.

We tend to focus on technological changes that have presumably made life easier, like computers, cell phones, and GPS units in cars, which sometimes distract us momentarily, blinding us to warnings flashing on our moral compasses. But without certain visionaries taking risks and acting in the world, we would be far worse off in many other ways. And the next decade will be shaped by the manifestations of people who are acting on their decisions and making changes today. We may not even be aware of many of those seeds that are being planted, but we will see the fruit ripen in the years to come.

The first three steps to manifesting change require a lot of interior work, fearless exploration, profound honesty. There's nothing easy about all that, even though much of the process is intuitive. Frankly, most of us in the West find intuitive activity to be hard work. A renowned Tibetan lama once pointed out that Westerners think people in the East are "lazy" because they tend to be more introspective and less concerned with material success (at least they were until recently). On the contrary, he felt that by keeping their minds constantly occupied with thinking and doing business, Westerners have avoided the harder effort of looking within.

Still, you could theoretically carry out the steps of looking, deciding, and connecting without leaving your home. Nothing wrong with that, mind you. The French philosopher Blaise Pascal once said, "I have discovered that all human evil comes from this, man's being unable to sit still in a room." Spending time alone in your room can be challenging in its own way.

But eventually the time comes to act, and that, as they say, is where the rubber meets the road. As Anaïs Nin wrote in her *Diary*, "Our life is composed greatly from dreams, from the unconscious, and they must be brought into connection with Action. They must be woven together." You need to connect to Source to have the strength and support to act, but you need to act before you can manifest change.

The two steps are interrelated, of course. Much of the planning and organizing of the civil rights movement of the 1950s and '60s took place in Southern churches, where prayer and singing combined with the traditional role of the black church as a community gathering place, credit union, people's court, support group, and center of political activism. Two of the movement's most important leaders, Martin Luther King, Jr., and Ralph Abernathy, were ministers. But the infusion of spiritual values affected most of the key players in that era of profound manifestation of social change.

"There's a sense in which the civil rights movement was the church in action," Andrew Young says in the documentary film *We Shall Not Be Moved* (2001). In 1961 Young had left his position as a pastor to work with the Southern Christian Leadership Conference, the church-centered civil rights organization led by King. "The civil rights movement was primarily a religious movement," adds the historian Wilson Fallin in the same film, "a movement of people who believed in God and who were convinced that God would help them overcome segregation." That sentiment was clearly shared by many in the movement that took shape in the black churches, such as Congressman John Lewis, who grew up in segregated Georgia and tasted firsthand the bitter fruits of racism and discrimination. "I saw hate," he says, "and I came to the conclusion that hate was too heavy a burden to bear. I felt called to do what I call 'get in the way,' to be maladjusted." In 1965 Lewis took part in the marches from Selma to Montgomery, Alabama, that marked the political and emotional peak of the voting rights movement there. During the first march, now known as Bloody Sunday, he was among the six hundred marchers who were attacked by state and local police with billy clubs and tear gas.

"I felt like I was participating in a holy march," he later said. "It was something so moving, so precious, so spiritual." Then he saw the troopers putting on gas masks and coming toward the column of peaceful marchers, beginning to beat the marchers and releasing tear gas. "I thought I was going to die," said Lewis, who was beaten so badly that he still bears the scars. "But we didn't fight back. We didn't strike back. We didn't hate. We had been taught to love. The way of love is much more powerful, much more creative. And somehow I came to realize that there was a spark of the Divine in every human being. And I didn't have a right to dislike, to despise, or to hate, or to strike out against that spark of the Divine. . . . I had to love."

When we act based on love rather than hate, the universe often finds surprising ways to support us. On the same day that the Bloody Sunday march was taking place, ABC-TV happened to be broadcasting Stanley Kramer's 1961 film *Judgment at Nuremberg*, a dramatization of the post–World War II Nuremberg trials of Nazi war criminals. That night many TV stations interrupted the film to show clips of the violence in Selma. Some viewers thought the footage of police in military-style helmets and riot gear brutally beating protesters was part of the film. "The violence in Selma was so similar to the violence in Nazi Germany that viewers could hardly miss the connection," wrote Andrew Young. Although the film was a reenactment, it was notable for including actual footage filmed by American soldiers after the liberation of the Nazi concentration camps. The horrific parallels weren't lost on the American public, which responded with an outpouring of support; thousands of people of all religions and races flocked to Selma to take part in the next march.

That kind of coincidence is just one more example of what King himself referred to in his final speech as "transphysics," meaning a transcending of normal principles of the material world. Talking about the infamous police official Bull Connor of Birmingham, Alabama, King noted that Connor would "send the dogs forth and they did come; but we just went before the dogs singing, 'Ain't gonna let nobody turn me round.' Bull Connor next would say, 'Turn the fire hoses on.'" But as King put it, "Bull Connor didn't know history. He knew a kind of physics that somehow didn't relate to the transphysics that we knew about. And that was the fact that there was a certain kind of fire that no water could put out."

That same principle of transphysics has uplifted the lives of many people less well known than John Lewis and Martin Luther King, Jr. When I was growing up in New York City, our next-door neighbor was a local fire chief, Joseph Miccio, who was a good friend of my father's. Chief Miccio's own father had been killed by a criminal in the line of duty as a police officer, yet Joseph did not become embittered. He spent his life saving lives and protecting property. He had the inherent qualities of a leader, the kind of person other firefighters would follow into a burning building when everyone else is running the other way. Joe Miccio manifested change in his life by overcoming the temptation to feel victimized and instead responding with love and courage to the apparently negative fate he had been dealt.

Not every action to manifest change requires the kind of physical sacrifice made by many people in the civil rights movement or by police and firefighters. Yet we know all too well that anyone seeking to manifest real change can expect opposition. As the great English satirist Jonathan Swift wrote, "When a true genius appears in the world, you may know him by this sign, that the dunces are all in confederacy against him." There is no shortage of transformational work to be done, from small personal or local changes to major revolutions. Never before has humanity needed more sacred activists to step up and do the work of changing the world. The great change agent Gandhi said it best: "It is the quality of our work which will please God, and not the quantity."

In his film *Fierce Light: When Spirit Meets Action*, Velcrow Ripper detailed the efforts of 350 residents of South Central Los Angeles to turn a patch of barren land into an inner-city garden. Through a decade of hard work and communal cooperation, they created an Eden in the midst of concrete and urban blight. When developers threatened to take back the land, which had been given to residents by the city of Los Angeles, a community formed to protest the action. The developers succeeded in evicting the neighborhood people from their garden oasis—but two years later the same group of farmers planted a new farm on eighty-five acres outside the city limits. Now they bring fresh organic produce to neighborhoods around the city and hold a farmers' market every month by the site of their original farm.

As the saying goes, we have to think globally while for the most part acting locally. Be aware that even a small action has the potential to drop a boulder into the collective consciousness of humanity and ripple out into the wider world. Gandhi began his paradigm-shifting work when he was still a fledgling lawyer sent to South Africa to argue cases involving civil rights abuses heaped on the community of Indian laborers living there in the early years of the twentieth century. For his troubles, Gandhi himself was subjected to similar abuses. When the magistrate of a court in Durban ordered Gandhi to remove his turban, he refused, and this simple act became a turning point in his life.

After returning to India, Gandhi organized protests by peasants, farmers, and urban laborers over excessive land taxes and discrimination imposed by their colonial rulers. That resistance led in time to nationwide campaigns to combat poverty, expand women's rights, and put an end to the country's own horrific prejudice against so-called untouchables, Indians of low birth who were outside the caste system. In the end, Gandhi succeeded in terminating British rule over India.

As momentous as that may seem, though, Gandhi's influence spread across continents and had a profound impact on the American civil rights movement. Despite being a minister, by his own admission Martin Luther King, Jr., had reached a stage at which he "despaired of the power of love in solving social problems." At that point, he was coincidentally introduced to the life of Gandhi in a sermon by Mordecai Johnson, president of Howard University, who had just returned from a trip to India. King began reading about Gandhi's transformative use of nonviolence as a political instrument against British colonial rule. "As I read,"

King later said, "I became deeply fascinated by his campaigns of nonviolent resistance. As I delved deeper into the philosophy of Gandhi, my skepticism concerning the power of love gradually diminished, and I came to see for the first time its potency in the area of social reform."

King did not see his dream made fully manifest, but his eyes saw the coming of the day. In the last speech he gave before he was assassinated, he spoke prophetically: "We've got some difficult days ahead, but it really doesn't matter with me now, because I've been to the mountaintop," he said. "I don't mind. Like anybody I would like to live a long life—longevity has its place. But I'm not concerned about that now. I just want to do God's will. And he's allowed me to go up to the mountain, and I've looked over, and I've seen the Promised Land. I may not get there with you, but I want you to know tonight that we as a people will get to the Promised Land. So I'm happy tonight, I'm not worried about anything. I'm not fearing any man. Mine eyes have seen the glory of the coming of the Lord."

And with those words ringing in the rafters of the church where he spoke in Memphis, Tennessee, he left the stage. I don't think people fully appreciate the genius of Martin Luther King, Jr.: He was a great being, an anchor of divine force on Earth, and one day he may be considered a saint as well.

I have been blessed with the privilege of restoring limbs and faces by connecting with this same divine force. Each time I look at a disfigured limb and hold the intention, even before it manifests, my inner eye has already seen the divine result.

We have all been given gifts. What we decide to do with those gifts is our gift to God, but how we act on them is our gift to humanity. We all have a choice to stand by and watch or to be among the noble spirits who manifest change on this planet for their larger family.

I will close this chapter with a story that I hope will inspire you to rise off your pillow, take the bellows to ignite the divine spark within you, and go out and manifest the change that your heart desires and your conscience decrees. The journalist J. A. Spender once proposed the following scenario: "You say that you'll act, if Mrs. S. and Mrs. B. will begin. If so, none of you will do anything. Have you never heard the story of the bewitched forest—how an evil spirit told all the trees that the first of them to blossom in the spring would be withered and destroyed, and how each of them waited for someone else to begin, and so the whole forest remained dark and dead for a thousand years?"

# Chapter 21

## STEP FIVE: MANIFEST

First they ignore you, then they laugh
at you, then they fight you, then you
win.

—Mohandas Gandhi

Never doubt that a small group of
thoughtful, committed citizens can
change the world. Indeed, it is the only
thing that ever has.

—Margaret Mead

**man·i·fest**

**adj.**

1. readily perceived by the eye or the understanding; evident;
   obvious; apparent; plain.
2. of or pertaining to conscious feelings, ideas, and impulses
   that contain repressed psychic material; the manifest con-

tent of a dream, as opposed to the latent content that it conceals.

**verb**

3. to make clear or evident to the eye or the understanding; show plainly.
4. to prove; put beyond doubt or question.

—dictionary.com

Manifesting, by definition, means bringing forth and making plain your dreams. You need to know that you are more than you have been led to believe. The playing field has changed, and more than one glass ceiling has been shattered.

As I drank my morning coffee one day while working on this book, I was listening to the news that a man of color had just been elected president of the United States. This landmark event struck me as being less about politics or race and more about the fact that, all around us, the world we live in represents the material manifestation of dreams. The Wright brothers' dream fills the skies with airplanes. Susan B. Anthony's dreams have changed the lot of millions of women. Mohandas Gandhi's dreams have transformed the fate of an entire nation. When I was nine and standing before the Wheel of Chance at that church fair, it seemed like the world was somehow lining up with my dream of getting a bicycle. Later, when I was seventeen, I felt a silent inner call to run down the beach with my lifeguard crew to answer a prayer that could not be read or received by the "normal" senses. Now, decades later, I wake up and the world I live in is the manifestation of the dreams of a long lineage of souls who got off their pillows to make change happen.

The dream I had as a teenager of pursuing a career in healthcare, trying to fit myself into the old paradigm of medicine, may not have manifested in that form; indeed, I couldn't see the top of the stairs when I took the first step in faith. But as I sat listening to the radio and marveling at all the changes wrought in the wider world, I realized that in my own world people were reaching out to me and that I was able to help them. When I first volunteered my services at Memorial Sloan-Kettering Cancer Center, the administrators there thanked me for applying but told me that they had no category they could put me in. As my friend Mitch had put it, I was uniquely qualified for a job yet to be created. But in helping the people I've described in the pages of this book, and many more as well, I had uncovered the secret to my own salvation. I had realized my heart's desire. Like Michelangelo manifesting an angel from a block of marble, I was manifesting the life of my dreams.

Yet I had to look back to see how all the pieces had been falling into place almost without my realizing it. The more closely I looked, the more surprising and intricate I realized many of those connections were—and sometimes the connections took the form of oppositions. The doctor I had consulted when I was questioning my work in real estate and feeling at sea in the world told me that the course of action was for him to prescribe drugs that might make the symptoms less prominent but would not cure the problem. Then a barefoot woman from South America looked at me and said, "There is nothing wrong with you. You're just not doing what you're supposed to be doing." What she meant was that I wasn't living aligned with my sacred purpose. She had no degree on her wall, no fancy office or other external markers that might indicate to the ordinary world that she was what they would call "a person of substance." But her second opinion was accurate and helped eliminate the symptoms I had been experiencing.

A short time later, having followed her advice and found the right path for myself, I was beginning to work with people in a small office I was leasing from a mapmaker. The only window faced a brick wall and fire escapes, but I was happy to be there. Each day when I walked from my home to my office, I would try to take a different route. One morning I walked up Second Avenue and stopped at a bagel shop off Fifty-sixth Street. I stepped out into the sun, paused for a moment, and put my coffee down to take off the lid. As I did, I observed the façade of a building that I hadn't noticed before. I was facing a small lawn decorated with shrubbery and azalea bushes, set back maybe fifty feet from the sidewalk between First and Second Avenues. Squirrels chased each other between the bushes, a host of robins bounced along looking for worms in the dewy morning grass, and pigeons pecked at the lawn. I stood there awhile, sipping my coffee and appreciating this lovely little oasis in the middle of Manhattan. I allowed myself to dream about how beneficial it would be to have a view like that. I imagined what wonderful work I could do if my eyes had the room to stretch and my soul to expand as I sat daily listening to people from all over the world sharing with me their obstacles that seemed to defy solution. Maybe someday, I thought.

A few days later Dr. Elizabeth Muss came to ask me to help her with her injured knee. The address on her card read "The Bristol Medical Building, 55th Street." In the course of our work together, Dr. Muss happened to ask me a question that seemed to come out of nowhere: Did I need a bigger office? She said she had just learned that an office would be opening in her building. I was planning to leave for Machu Picchu at the end of the week, but I had intended to look for a new office upon my return. I said I'd love to check it out. She handed me a card with the number of the doctor who was leasing the office and said I should speak to her about it. When I called the woman, she asked me, "What kind of physician are you?"

"I'm not a doctor," I said. "I work for a medical education and research foundation, composed of a cross-disciplinary group of healthcare professionals." That satisfied her, and she agreed to show me the office the following day. When I arrived at the building, I walked down a long hallway, took an elevator, then walked down another hallway until I reached the office number I had written on the card. The doctor opened the door to the vacant office and invited me to have a look. A large picture window on the far side caught my attention, and I crossed the space to take in the view: I was looking out at a lush lawn with pigeons and squirrels and azalea bushes in bloom. It was the little oasis that I had paused to appreciate and dream about a few weeks before! "I'll take it," I said.

"Wouldn't you like to know how much it is?" she said.

"No," I said. "I'm sure it's fine. I'll take it." And I signed a lease for three years.

I mentioned earlier that while I was in the maritime college, I learned something fascinating about ships—that you can tell the magnitude of a vessel by the size of the wake it leaves, even after it has passed from view. But there's something else about a ship's wake. When I was a midshipman, we sailed through the roughest seas. As I stood on the fantail and looked back at the wake of the training ship the *Empire State*, I felt that it created a smooth sea in its path. While I was still living on Long Island, my dad and I left the house one morning to go across the bay in his boat. It was a raw, windy day, and the water was rough and choppy, but I wasn't worried, because I knew my dad would have a way to handle it. Then I noticed a group of small boats in the harbor, just kind of moving around in circles, marking time. I asked Dad what they were doing. He told me that they were waiting for a big boat to leave the marina and set sail for the mainland, creating a smooth wake that they could follow.

In a way, that's what the great manifesters do. They leave a legacy, a path for others to follow. By their courage, their strength in the face of all odds, they create big, smooth wakes through the rough water. The Gandhis, the Kings, the Wright brothers, and other leaders and visionaries smooth the way for the rest of us to follow. But what we need to understand is that we all have that same potential to create wakes that can smooth the way for others and leave lasting benefits. Sometimes those others may consist of our families, our local communities, our colleagues at work, or maybe just one other person—a spouse or partner, a parent or child, a friend in need. But as we manifest our change, the wakes we leave behind spread out just as a boat's wake does on the surface of the water. We start out by changing our lives and the lives of loved ones, and then they change someone's life, and the effect ripples outward until many more people are affected by what we have manifested.

Because my high school guidance counselor couldn't see the potential in me, and couldn't measure the passion in my heart to serve in healthcare, he probably took it upon himself to dash my dreams on the rocks of his rational mind and summarily label me as an underachiever. Now, as I sit in my office reading letters asking me to lecture at universities around the world, and to collaborate with leading pioneers in medicine, I get a chuckle out of the brilliance of Einstein, who said, "Whoever undertakes to set himself up as a judge of Truth and Knowledge is shipwrecked by the laughter of the gods."

The old worldview of judging someone's worth or potential based on external appearances, pedigree, or test-taking ability is flawed because it neglects the real potential that exists in the soul. Because of my own early experiences in school, I was especially moved when I discovered the story of Vivien Thomas and Alfred Blalock. Coming of age in Nashville, Tennessee, in the 1920s, Thomas dreamed of becoming a doctor. Although he was an African American in a segregated city, because Nashville had a thriving black middle class, Thomas received a solid high school education, graduating with honors. But as he was preparing to enter college and pursue a career in medicine, the stock market crash of 1929 and the ensuing Depression wiped out his savings and made that goal seem impossible.

Not to be dissuaded from his dream, Thomas took a job as a lab technician at Vanderbilt University's medical school. There he had the good fortune of working for Alfred Blalock, an established surgeon and medical researcher. Although Dr. Blalock shared some of the prejudices of his time and place, he was quick to realize that Thomas had a natural aptitude not only for research but also for performing intricate surgical procedures. By practicing on dogs, Thomas developed the surgical operations that eventually led to a groundbreaking procedure to cure a congenital heart disease. Because the country wasn't ready for a black surgeon, Dr. Blalock performed the actual surgeries while Thomas guided him by standing on a step stool and looking over his shoulder! Strange as it may seem, cardiac surgery itself was taboo at the time they began experimenting with this and other procedures, so more than one barrier was being torn down by this historic collaboration.

Blalock gained great acclaim when he moved to Johns Hopkins—but only after insisting that Vivien Thomas come with him and be put on the payroll there. Baltimore was more harshly segregated than Nashville, though, so Thomas had to be placed on the janitorial payroll. When he was seen walking the halls of the august institution dressed in a white lab coat, it created an uproar. In time, though, Thomas received the recognition he was due, and after Blalock's death he took on a new role mentoring the first generation of African American medical students at Johns Hopkins. This is where his actions manifested an even wider legacy. In the words of Dr. Levi Watkins, Jr., of Johns Hopkins, Vivien Thomas is "the most untalked about, unappreciated, unknown giant in the African-American community. What he helped facilitate impacted people all over the world."

Thomas not only helped open doors in the medical and surgical professions for African Americans but also paved the way for future inventions and technologies that have helped surgeons and patients of all races and backgrounds. One of the surgical students Thomas taught was Rowena Spencer, a white woman who faced great resistance because of her gender yet who, like Thomas, rose above the prevailing prejudice to carve out a legacy of her own. "Many times in my career I was complimented on my surgical technique," Dr. Spencer said, "and I will admit that a good many people were shocked when I told them I learned my surgical technique from a black man who had only a high school education."

The story of Thomas and Blalock is eloquently told in the film *Partners of the Heart*, based on Thomas's autobiography, which was published just after he died. Perhaps my favorite moment in his career occurred after Thomas executed an especially difficult surgical procedure so flawlessly that Blalock, marveling at the nearly undetectable suture line, said, "Vivien, are you sure you did this? This looks like something the Lord made."

These two great heretics together broke the centuries-old myth of medicine that said the heart could not be touched, even by a surgeon. It was long feared that the soul resided in the heart, and so people believed that that organ should never be handled—just as today many doctors hold on to the myth that Mind resides in the brain.

Many doctors but, fortunately, not all. In November 2007, several members of the Global Health Institute's board received invitations to attend the inaugural Pioneers of Integrative Medicine award event, held at the Grand Hyatt in Manhattan and hosted by the Bravewell Collaborative, a group of foundations and philanthropists dedicated to advancing integrative medicine. This groundbreaking event was created to honor six of the leaders in that field, whose work in the 1980s and '90s paved the way for a new era in American healthcare.

The master of ceremonies was Dr. Mehmet Oz, who had become a household name because of his appearances on a popular TV show and a series of best-selling books. The honorees made up a virtual hall of fame of integrative practitioners: Dean Ornish, James Gordon, Jon Kabat-Zinn, Andrew Weil, Larry Dossey, and Rachel Naomi Remen. All are medical doctors except Kabat-Zinn, who received a Ph.D. in molecular biology from MIT, where he studied under Salvador Luria, a Nobel laureate in medicine. Of the six, the only one who may not be known to most readers is Dr. Remen, the cofounder and medical director of the Commonweal Cancer Help Program, which has cared for people with cancer and their families for almost thirty years.

Although Dr. Remen was also the only woman so honored, I couldn't help noticing that the majority of people in the room championing this sea change in medical consciousness were themselves women. That included the chair of Bravewell, Christy Mack, who, as the daughter of a family doctor in Greensboro, North Carolina, grew up watching her father treat patients in their home.

As I walked to the street after the ceremony and flagged a taxi, I thought of the words of Max Planck, the Nobel laureate who ushered in the concept of quantum physics that had opened the conceptual doors for all of us to walk through. "A new scientific truth does not triumph by convincing its opponents and making them see the light," Planck wrote, "but rather because its opponents eventually die, and a new generation grows up that is familiar with it." (His words are often condensed to the catchier saying that "science advances one funeral at a time"!) I felt as though I had just witnessed the collective birth of that next generation of leaders who were manifesting the "new scientific truth" that would eventually triumph. I felt a deep gratitude for having been invited to that ceremony and being given the opportunity to meet this kindred group of women and men engaged in advancing the integration of healthcare.

When people ask me the difference between the fourth and fifth steps—between acting and manifesting—I sometimes say that it may take a prolonged act, or several actions, to manifest a lasting result. That's what makes great manifesters like William Wilberforce, the Wright brothers, Mahatma Gandhi, Martin Luther King, Jr., and Vivien Thomas so extraordinary. They had to maintain their focus through disappointments, setbacks, and personal attacks. While I was struggling in my pioneering work, a respected colleague sent me the following quotation from the eighteenth-century British statesman and author Edmund Burke. "There is a sort of enthusiasm in all projectors," he wrote, "absolutely necessary for their affairs, which makes them proof against the most fatiguing delays, the most mortifying disappointments, the most shocking insults; and, what is severer than all, the presumptuous judgment of the ignorant upon their designs."

I can't say often enough, however, that to manifest change in the world you don't have to be a political activist or a pioneer in healthcare. Many manifesters were ordinary people who changed some aspect of culture we don't normally think of as revolutionary. Many gifts are still reserved for future generations to open, along with countless applications by which you can manifest your unique gift. It needn't be grandiose, obvious, or earth-shaking.

But there is something else of significance you need to know about the Five Steps that I've laid out here. You may think at first blush that this is a finite process—that is, once you look, decide, connect, act, and manifest, you're done. Nothing could be further from the truth. Some religious traditions, for example, teach what I would consider a bogus version of the goal of sacred empowerment: that, once you are "ignited" or "enlightened" or "liberated" or "sealed" (choose your own terminology), nothing more is required of you. But the wisest spiritual masters and teachers know that just the opposite is true. To a one they have taught that genuine realization manifests as a desire to be of service. And, clearly, service is an ongoing manifestation. Discovering your gift, igniting your sacred potential, acting on it, and manifesting change does not mean that all your problems are solved, although it does mean you're finally on the right path.

Jack Kornfield wrote about this phenomenon in his wonderfully titled book *After the Ecstasy, the Laundry*. There's a famous Zen saying: "Before enlightenment, chop wood and carry water. After enlightenment, chop wood and carry water." Kornfield interviewed hundreds of spiritual practitioners from a wide range of traditions and discovered that, even after having had the most mystical experiences, and having taught their insights in many cases for decades, they can still be faced with the day-to-day task of maintaining the freedom they've discovered. "Most spiritual accounts end with illumination or enlightenment," Kornfield writes. "But what if we ask what happens after that? What happens when the Zen master returns home to spouse and children? What happens when the Christian mystic goes shopping? . . . How do we live our understanding with a full heart?"

Much the same is true of igniting your sacred potential and manifesting a change you want to see in the world. You will need to maintain your focus, remember what inspired you to manifest change in the first place, and continue to fight for what you believe. My hope is that many of you who read this book will have the courage to leave the safety of the known and adventure into the new. I also hope that my journey may serve to smooth the waters just a little to help you on your own journey to explore the potential waiting in your soul to be ignited. You have the power. You have what it takes to transform the world. You have within you a gift that will allow you to make manifest in the world the change you want to see. I promise you that this is true. This is a promise that God has made to us in the sacred texts of all the great traditions, and it is a promise that science is now beginning to embrace. The sacred potential of humanity is making itself felt in all fields of human endeavor and inviting us on the most profound journey. As Gandhi wrote, "The difference between what we do and what we are capable of doing would suffice to solve most of the world's problems."

Above all, keep in mind the old nautical saying, "A ship in the harbor is safe, but that is not what ships are made for." Setting out from your safe harbor requires not only courage but also a commitment of time and energy over the long haul. So it really helps to have a group of like-minded souls who can support you and share the work. Fortunately, a growing body of people has begun to see that a change of consciousness is blooming. We are nearing a tipping point, when the strength of the evidence, and the number of people who have already experienced what I have written about in this book, will help manifest it in the world as a day-to-day reality.

Another great visionary, although less well known than Gandhi, was a Jesuit priest and paleontologist named Pierre Teilhard de Chardin. "Someday after we have mastered the sky, the waves, the tides, and gravity," he wrote, "we shall harness for God the energies of love. Then for the second time in the history of the world, man will have discovered fire."

The greatest privilege of all teachers is to see their students excel beyond their own achievement. I know that my students will surpass what I have done. I wish to thank you in advance, as I know that some of you will leave a legacy in the form of an invention, a book, an improvement, a masterpiece, a solution that the world is waiting for and that you were born to manifest.

# ACKNOWLEDGMENTS

I am tremendously grateful for the friends, family, events, and obstacles that preceded that moment a decade ago in my quiet basement restoration studio, when my mind was unshackled long enough to dream with the joy of a child. That moment set in motion a chain of events that transformed my consciousness and led to transforming the bodies of those I worked with. It also irrevocably altered the minds of the scientists, doctors, and theologians with whom I was brought into contact and ultimately led me to encounter the enlightened literary agent, publisher, entertainment attorney, and writers who helped in the manifestation of this book.

But where to fairly give credit to those who shaped my life is a daunting question—like which came first, the chicken or the egg? So I shall do my best to acknowledge publicly those whose names I can remember and ask those I may have forgotten to forgive me my trespass.

To my mom, Carol, a wonderful artist and gifted gardener, who demonstrated in word and deed the value of empathy and unfailing affection during my childhood. When I struggled with an undiagnosed learning disability that wreaked havoc and confusion on my peripatetic journey to find my path in life, you were a virtual life raft that kept me afloat in my earliest years and taught me lessons that have served me well as an adult.

To my dad, Jack, a giant of a man who demonstrated by example, striding on the roof of a burning building as a New York firefighter, rescuing creatures large and small—from adults and children who had succumbed to smoke to showing respect for all forms of life by pausing on the roof of an inferno to pick up a stranded wet kitten and give it safe passage on his wide shoulders down a ladder before the building was consumed by flames. Even his rugged maverick attitude in print and TV commercials, whether riding a horse as an American cowboy or dashing into action as a Royal Canadian Mountie, conveyed to me the value of courage and action in the face of adversity.

To the great leaders I have had the pleasure of meeting and/or corresponding with over the years, who have done so much to advance the recognition and integration of Mind-Body-Spirit and the efficacious potential of consciousness to effect healing of the human body, the body politic, and social ills, I offer thanks: John E. Mack, Patricia A. Muehsam, Theresa Hale, Dean Radin, Beverly Rubik, Robert Jahn, Deepak Chopra, Caroline Myss, Marilyn M. Schlitz, Audrey Kitagawa, Larry Scherwitz, Ron Navarre, Jampa Mackenzie Stewart, the Dalai Lama, Master C. K. Chu, Patricia Carrington, Lynne McTaggart, Russell ("the Professor") Berke, Eric Pearl, Frederic Brussat, Alan Steinfeld, Rudolph Ballentine, Stan Grof, Peter Roche de Coppens, Catherine Crier; my cospeakers at the Aspen Health and Wellness Forum, Gary Schwartz, and Christiane Northrup; the inspirational participants of the 2007 Bravewell Pioneers in Integrative Medicine Awards: Larry Dossey, James Gordon, Mehmet Oz, Andrew Weil, and Dean Ornish. All are enlightened pioneers who at one time in their lives suffered the slings and arrows of ignorance and censure in advancing the evolution of humanity, but whose intellectual, physical, and spiritual footprints smoothed a path to assist me in gaining a foothold a decade ago, when I dared to follow my heart's desire regardless of "common" wisdom.

I owe a special debt of gratitude to those figures who made this book a reality. The perceptive and charismatic Jan Miller, president of Dupree Miller & Associates literary agency, who discovered my story and had the faith to back me as a first-time author; and to Nena Madona at Dupree Miller, who was a wonderful help. To the vision of Judith Curr at Atria Books, who is manifesting paradigm-altering books that are assisting in the evolution of humanity; and, of course, my editor, Sarah Durand, whose skill and diplomacy were integral in producing the manuscript. And thanks to Sarah Cantin, who helped orchestrate this book like a world-class conductor.

To my cowriter, the vastly talented Peter Occhiogrosso, who worked above and beyond the call of duty to make this book possible, reaching out to persons illustrated in the book to get a firsthand picture of their beliefs and experiences encountering the miraculous in a technologically dominant world, and especially for his profound work on the chapter Building the Bridge. To Alison Draper, a magically gifted writer who helped me describe the events in my life in a cinematic way, to help readers feel as if they were actually on the beach with me, or in the clinical setting where these events transpired. She is a true godsend.

To the talented wordsmith James Twiford, who was profoundly helpful to me as a new writer shaping the preliminary draft during the proposal stage.

To the tremendously talented and award-winning filmmaker Marc Wishengrad at Wishengrad Pictures, who filmed my work over the past decade and, with the help of Christy Musumecci and Alison Draper, captured the interviews of the physicians who testified to what they saw firsthand, so their words could be transcribed to support the book.

To the pro bono team of lawyers at Global Health Institute, first of whom I must single out Armand Fried, who after observing me work with a participant donated many hours of his time to watch my back, keep a roof over my head, and keep the barbarians at the gate during the decade of virtually unpaid research for Global Health Institute.

In gratitude to the past and present Chairs of the Medical Advisory Board at the Global Health Institute, John E. Mack, M.D.; Frank Salvatore, M.D.; and Len Horovitz, M.D., whose past and present work continues to advance the integration of healthcare. And in recognition of the altruistic spirit of the Chair of the Board of Trustees at the Global Health Institute, David M. Coiro.

To the wonderful team of media experts at Reel Potential Media, who did a tremendous job with the marketing material for *Manifesting Michelangelo*. With special gratitude to Paige MacKenzie Welborn, a rising star in media.

And I offer immense gratitude to the consummate entertainment attorney Marc Jacobson, who was instrumental in bringing this literary project to fruition, and who continues to guide me with his broad experience in producing inspirational media in all forms.

And perhaps more important than any other influence, I would have to single out my father, who later in life instilled in me the belief that with a little faith one could move mountains, and I believed him.

In contemporary society, the role models in the physical world—the civil rights leaders and political statesmen—and those in the virtual "reel" world of media, who step up and do the right thing, are few and far between, yet we need to be reminded that if only we act on our inspirations, hope remains to do good. The iconic actor Clint Eastwood once said, "Every good thing I ever achieved, I was advised against doing." As I look back, I find it true that while it is important to have reverence for the past and for the giants who went before us, it is equally, if not more, important to benefit from their work and then set forth to carve out the life you were born to manifest.

JPF/NYC 2011

# SELECTED BIBLIOGRAPHY

## BOOKS

Ballentine, Rudolph. *Radical Healing: Integrating the World's Great Therapeutic Traditions to Create a New Transformative Medicine.* New York: Three Rivers, 2000.

Borysenko, Joan, and Miroslav Borysenko. *The Power of the Mind to Heal: Renewing Body, Mind, and Spirit.* Carlsbad, Calif: Hay House, 1994.

Braden, Gregg. *The Spontaneous Healing of Belief: Shattering the Paradigm of False Limits.* Carlsbad, Calif.: Hay House, 2009.

———. *The Divine Matrix: Bridging Time, Space, Miracles, and Belief.* Carlsbad, Calif.: Hay House, 2007.

Brown, Dan. *The Lost Symbol.* New York: Doubleday, 2009.

Brussat, Frederic, and Mary Ann Brussat. *Spiritual Literacy: Reading the Sacred in Everyday Life.* New York: Scribner, 1998.

Burke, Edmund. *An Account of the European Settlements in America.* Nabu Press, 2010. (Orig. pub. 1757)

Campbell, Joseph, with Bill Moyers. *The Power of Myth.* New York: Doubleday, 1988.

Chopra, Deepak. *The Seven Spiritual Laws of Success: A Practical Guide to the Fulfillment of Your Dreams.* Novato, Calif.: New World Library, 1994.

———. *Quantum Healing: Exploring the Frontiers of Mind/Body Medicine.* New York: Bantam, 1990.

Dossey, Larry. *Reinventing Medicine: Beyond Mind-Body to a New Era of Healing.* San Francisco: HarperSanFrancisco, 1999.

———. *Healing Words: The Power of Prayer and the Practice of Medicine.* New York: HarperOne, 1997.

Dyer, Wayne W. *The Power of Intention.* Carlsbad, Calif.: Hay House, 2005.

———. *There's a Spiritual Solution to Every Problem.* New York: Harper Paperbacks, 2003.

Feather, William. *The Business of Life.* New York: Simon & Schuster, 1949.

Gandhi, Mohandas K. *An Autobiography: The Story of My Experiments with Truth.* Translated by Mahadev Desai. Boston: Beacon Press, 1993. (Orig. pub. 1929.)

Gordon, James S. *Unstuck: Your Guide to the Seven-Stage Journey Out of Depression.* New York: Penguin, 2009.

———. *Manifesto for a New Medicine: Your Guide to Healing Partnerships and the Wise Use of Alternative Therapies.* Reading, Mass.: Addison-Wesley, 1997.

Jahn, Robert G., and Brenda J. Dunne. *Margins of Reality: The Role of Consciousness in the Physical World.* New York: Harcourt Brace, 1997.

McTaggart, Lynne. *The Field: The Quest for the Secret Force of the Universe.* Updated ed. New York: Harper, 2008.

———. *The Intention Experiment: Using Your Thoughts to Change Your Life and the World.* New York: Free Press, 2007.

Myss, Caroline. *Anatomy of the Spirit: The Seven Stages of Power and Healing.* New York: Three Rivers Press, 1996.

———. *Sacred Contracts: Awakening Your Divine Potential.* New York: Three Rivers Press, 2003.

Radin, Dean. *The Conscious Universe: The Scientific Truth of Psychic Phenomena.* San Francisco: HarperOne, 2009. (Orig. pub. 1997.)

Reik, Theodor. *Listening with the Third Ear: The Inner Experience of a Psychoanalyst.* New York: Farrar, Straus and Giroux, 1983. (Orig. pub. 1948.)

Schiltz, Marilyn, and Tina Amorok, with Marc S. Micozzi. *Consciousness and Healing: Integral Approaches to Mind-Body Medicine.* New York: Churchill Livingstone, 2004.

Sheldrake, Rupert. *The Sense of Being Stared At, and Other Aspects of the Extended Mind.* New York: Crown, 2003.

Stannard, Russell, ed. *God for the 21st Century.* Philadelphia: Templeton Foundation Press, 2000.

Vaughn-Lee, Llewellyn. *Light of Oneness.* Point Reyes Station, Calif.: Golden Sufi Center, 2004.

Williamson, Marianne. *A Return to Love: Reflections on the Principles of a Course in Miracles.* New York: HarperCollins, 1992.

Zukav, Gary. *The Dancing Wu Li Masters: An Overview of the New Physics.* San Francisco: HarperOne, 2001.

———. *The Seat of the Soul.* New York: Free Press, 1990.

## FILMOGRAPHY

*Fierce Light: When Spirit Meets Action.* Directed by Velcrow Ripper. Alive Mind, 2009.

*Partners of the Heart: American Experience.* Directed by Bill Duke and Andrea Kalin. PBS, 2003.

*We Shall Not Be Moved.* Directed by Bernie Hargis. Vision Video, 2001.

Made in the USA
Columbia, SC
27 November 2020